Dear Andy!

You can re live Italy! (in food)

Happy Birthday

xx

# My Italian Kitchen

## Victor Scerri

# My Italian Kitchen

NEW
HOLLAND

# Victor Scerri

Published in 2014
New Holland Publishers
London • Sydney • Auckland

First published in 2012
www.newhollandpublishers.com

The Chandlery Unit 114, 50 Westminster Bridge Road, London SE1 7QY, United Kingdom
1/66 Gibbes Street Chatswood NSW 2067 Australia
218 Lake Road Northcote Auckland New Zealand

Images: Page 73—Victor Scerri, page 22, 63, 69, 91 109, 129, 139, 165—Istock,
        page 28, 33, 77—Shutterstock.

A catalogue record of this book is available at the British Library and
the National Library of Australia.

ISBN: 9781742576091

Managing director: Fiona Schultz
Publisher: Linda Williams
Publishing director: Lliane Clarke
Editor: Simona Hill
Project editor: Jodi De Vantier
Designer: Tracy Loughlin
Food photographer: Graeme Gillies
Production director: Olga Dementiev
Printer: Toppan Leefung Printing Limited

10 9 8 7 6 5 4 3 2 1

Follow New Holland Publishers on
Facebook: www.facebook.com/NewHollandPublishers

This book is dedicated to my parents, Carmel and Anthony, to my nonna, and in memory of my nonno for all of their constant love, support, encouragement and belief in me.

# Foreword

Living in a rural area, I was always meeting wonderful families and almost immediately when the Scerri family acquired the property adjoining my own, a genuine sense of welcoming and warmth fell across our pretty rural village.

Victor was seven years old when I spotted him helping his grandfather tend to a remarkable garden. It was full of amazing tomatoes (still to this day are the very best I've ever eaten) that glowed with the spirit in which they were grown—as well as zucchini, eggplant, chillies, herbs all as equal. The produce became the staple of the Scerri's cooking, and with the predominate winds gently transferring aromas across the valley, I made it a point to get to know our new friends much closer.

As the years passed and I became more a family member than a friend, I would care for Victor and make him special treats after school. Victor was a charmer and even as a child he would be the first to open a door or offer a compliment, but it was his enthusiasm for food that caught my interest. Initially in eating it, and then in dedicated interest, he would question me on recipes, ingredients, methods, and even on topics like what was good at the restaurant this week!

During a period when I managed some of the largest catering events in the country was when Victor got his first opportunity in a restaurant kitchen. Victor was 15 and within months of washing dishes, scrubbing floors and the like he was prepping and then short order cooking. Victor was considered a senior chef long before he had an apprenticeship and I firmly believe that this period of long, hard labour, is why Victor has created his successes of today.

Victor would tell me all the time as we drove to those events 'I'm going to buy my first car with cash and have my own restaurant one day' and I never doubted him. Victor's personal drive to succeed in cooking and business is his strength. Coupled with a charismatic loyalty to his customers, family and friends, he has created his own recipe for happiness.

Victor is now in the best place of his life having gained the respect of his peers, being surrounded by his family in their restaurant everyday and not resting on his achievements. Victor is now embarking on a journey to even greater culinary heights and this book is his way of thanking you, the reader.

Enjoy this book and, as you prepare one of the many traditional Italian favourites, let your imagination drift into the Scerri family kitchen and you will understand just how devoted Victor is to helping you re-create his classics.

*Sharyn Johnstone*

# Contents

# Introduction

I've been inspired to share my favourite recipes with you in this book because cooking the annual season's greatest produce picked straight from the garden and paddock has become my passion—there isn't anything fresher in taste and presentation. Fresh produce means tasty food! I aim to inspire you to join me through the seasons and become a self-sufficient cook.

From the age of eight, I wanted to be in charge of a kitchen. Having grown up around a warm, loving family kitchen I developed a love and passion for eating and creating Italian and Mediterranean dishes.

Graduating as a Chef in 2004, I completed a butchery course on the side and now make my own sausages and salami's, which I use in the recipes created and served at my restaurant Vic's Cucina and Bar.

I hone my culinary skills and gather inspiration from my very talented and creative family and previous employers. I have also had the opportunity to gather inspiration while travelling, particularly while working at Il Cantonino (Perugia, Italy). Now, I eagerly set out to continue creating and perfecting my family–inspired recipes passed down the generations.

I am hopelessly devoted to pleasing everyone I prepare a meal for, by blending some history and passion, with Italian and Mediterranean flavours. Preferring to use local produce, home-grown and produced in the old style, I love to create wholesome feasts that will definitely satisfy. I prefer to cook with produce freshly picked from my garden and farmers from the local district, served with locally grown and harvested wines to encourage my customers to come back regularly.

Thanks to my chef's Robert Dimovski and John Winston Ninon and my kitchen staff. Very special thanks goes out to those who have taught and inspired me along the way, especially my Mum and Nonna who should take the credit for my passions and achievements.

If you're a cheerful carnivore or your eyes are bigger than your bellies and you want to tuck into your plates, proceed with pleasure and confidence and join me on this seasonal journey. I hope it will also inspire you too!

*Victor Scerri*

# Entrées

# BRUSCHETTA

Mix all ingredients together and serve on top of toasted ciabatta bread.

*Serves 3*

2 large ripe tomatoes, finely diced

1 small Spanish (Bermuda) onion, peeled and finely diced

4 fresh basil leaves, thinly sliced

20 ml (4 teaspoons) good quality balsamic vinegar

50 ml (2 fl oz) extra virgin olive oil

¼ clove garlic, peeled and very finely chopped

Salt and freshly ground black pepper

3 slices toasted ciabatta bread, to serve

*Traditionally, panna cotta is associated with sweet flavours. During my parents' travels to Sweden, they came across a savoury version and thought we could adapt the flavours with what we had in our garden back home. We knew the mild aniseed flavours of chervil would go well with the light and creamy cheese texture and the smoked salmon and roe.*

# CHERVIL PANNA COTTA

*Serves 4*

500 ml (16 fl oz) pouring
   (half-and-half) cream
250 ml (8 fl oz) chicken stock
½ cup chervil washed, dried
   and finely chopped
¼ teaspoon salt
¼ teaspoon white pepper
   powder
4 gelatine leaves
4 dariole moulds
Non-stick cooking spray, to
   coat
200 g (7 oz) smoked salmon
100 g (3½ oz) salmon roe

Put the cream, chicken stock and chervil into a large pan over medium heat and bring to a simmer. Reduce to a low heat and cook for 20 minutes stirring constantly. The low heats infuses the liquid with the chervil. Add the salt and pepper.

To prepare the gelatine, put the leaves in a small bowl of cold water according to the packet instructions, until soft, about 5 minutes. The gelatine will turn translucent when it is soft. Remove from the water and squeeze out the excess.

Add the gelatine to the cream and chicken stock liquid and stir well until the gelatine dissolves, 1–2 minutes.

Spray dariole moulds with non-stick cooking spray and pour the liquid into the moulds. Refrigerate to set for at least 6 hours.

To remove the panna cotta from the moulds, place the fingers gently on top of the panna cotta, pulling it away from the side of the mould. Turn out onto serving plates and serve surrounded by smoked salmon and topped with salmon roe. Serve with toasted ciabatta bread. This dish can be stored in the refrigerator for up to four days.

*This is a very easy and tasty dip you can prepare for your dinner party guests and serve with your favourite crackers or fresh vegetable sticks.*

# SALMON DIP

410 g (14 oz) can red salmon, drained

250 g (9 oz) cream (farmer's) cheese

115 g (4 oz/½ cup) mayonnaise

Juice of 1 lemon

60 ml (4 tablespoons) sour cream

3 gherkins, chopped

1 tablespoon chives, finely chopped

Freshly ground black pepper

Blend all the ingredients together in food processor for 40–50 seconds until evenly combined and finely chopped.

Decant into a serving dish or bowl. Cover with cling wrap and it will keep refrigerated for up to four days.

Serve with crusty bread or your favourite crackers.

*You can buy salted fish roe paste from any specialty supermarkets, continental delicatessens or specialty fish mongers. The ingredients of the fish roe vary depending on the brands you buy. Serve with crackers or toasted bread.*

# TARAMASALATA

Soak the bread in water, then squeeze out the excess moisture with your hands.

Put the fish roe paste and the drained bread in a mortar and pestle with 5 ml (1 teaspoon) of the oil and pound to combine.

Continue to add olive oil 15 ml (1 tablespoon) at a time until all the oil is added and the roe, oil and bread have become paste-like. Add the lemon juice and salt and pepper and continue to stir until combined.

Sprinkle with parsley when it's finished. Serve at room temperature and it can be stored in an air-tight container for up to three days.

1½ cups fresh white bread (remove crusts)
½ cup salted fish roe paste
1½ cups olive oil
Juice of 1 large lemon
Salt and pepper
1 teaspoon parsley, finely chopped

*Semi-dried tomatoes are softer than dried tomatoes and widely available from supermarkets and delicatessens. Serve with oysters.*

# SEMI-DRIED TOMATO AND OLIVE SALSA

Mix all ingredients except for the oil in a bowl and stir well to combine. Add a splash of extra virgin olive oil and mix well. Set aside for at least 30 minutes.

Spoon the ingredients over the oysters.

*Serves 2*

15 pieces semi-dried tomatoes, finely diced

150 g (5 oz) pitted green olives, finely diced

1 lime, zest and juice

½ medium Spanish (Bermuda) onion, peeled and finely diced

½ bunch coriander (cilantro), finely chopped

½ teaspoon caster (superfine) sugar

125 ml (4 oz/½ cup) extra virgin olive oil

12 oysters, to serve

*This is a delicious dish of baked, cheesy oysters.*

# OYSTERS WITH SMOKED SALMON AND CAMEMBERT CHEESE

*Serves 2*

250 g (9 oz/generous 1 cup) Camembert cheese, sliced

12 oysters, shucked

250 g (9 oz) smoked salmon

50 g (2 oz) fresh chives, finely chopped

Preheat the oven to 180°C/350°F/Gas Mark 4. Put the oysters on a baking sheet.

Evenly distribute the smoked salmon over the top of the oysters, then repeat with the cheese.

Bake for 10 minutes, or until the cheese turns golden. Garnish with chopped chives.

*For those who don't like raw seafood, this dish is a tasty alternative that won't seem like you've swallowed a mouthful of the ocean.*

# CRUMBED OYSTERS

Shuck the oysters and carefully remove them from their shell.

Wash the oyster shells and dry them thoroughly. Put on a tray and set aside.

Pour the flour into a small bowl and lightly coat the oysters. Shake off the excess.

To make an egg wash, in a small bowl, whisk the milk with the eggs and the garlic salt until combined. Put the breadcrumbs in a third bowl, add the Parmesan cheese and parsley, season with salt and pepper and mix well.

Dip the floured oysters in the egg wash, then roll in the breadcrumbs until thoroughly coated. Repeat this step so that oysters are double crumbed.

Heat the oil in a frying pan over a medium heat, then shallow-fry the oysters for approximately 30 seconds each side. Remove from the pan using a slotted spoon and place briefly on kitchen paper to remove the excess fat. Put each cooked oyster in a cleaned shell to serve. Serve with a dash of Caesar dressing on top of each oyster.

*Serves 2*

12 oysters

50 g (2 oz/⅓ cup) plain (all-purpose) flour

120 ml (4 fl oz/½ cup) milk

2 eggs

1 teaspoon garlic salt

50 g (2 oz/½ cup) breadcrumbs

50 g (2 oz/⅔ cup) Parmesan cheese, grated

5 sprigs parsley, finely chopped

Salt and ground black pepper

5 tablespoons vegetable oil, for frying

Vic's Caesar Dressing, to serve (see Sauces, Stocks & Dressings)

*This is another tasty version of baked oysters, a real treat for people who don't want to feel like they've swallowed a mouthful of the ocean.*

# OYSTERS PARMIGIANA

*Serves 2*

12 oysters, shucked

235ml (8¼ fl oz/1 cup) Napoli sauce (see Pasta)

200 g (7 oz) provolone cheese, grated (shredded)

1 tablespoon parsley, finely chopped

Preheat the oven to 180°C/350°F/Gas Mark 4.

Evenly divide the Napoli sauce over 12 oysters.

Scatter the cheese evenly over the top of each oyster.

Put on a baking sheet and bake in the oven for 10 minutes, or until the cheese is golden brown.

*When making this recipe, the quality of your calamari is of utmost importance. Your calamari mustn't smell fishy and to purchase the best quality means you need to trust your fish monger. You will need a deep-fryer for this recipe.*

# SALT AND PEPPER CALAMARI

Clean the calamari tubes. Butterfly them by slicing the tube lengthways. The calamari tubes should now lie flat. Score the calamari, on the diagonal, in a criss-cross pattern. Cut the scored calamari into 1.5 cm (½ in) strips and set aside.

Using a whisk, combine the flours in a large bowl. Dip the calamari strips into the flour a few and a time until completely coated. Shake off the excess flour.

Heat the oil in a deep fryer to 180°C/350°F/Gas Mark 4 and deep-fry the calamari strips in batches of five at a time for 1–1½ minutes, or until golden brown. Do not overcook the calamari or it will become tough. Put the cooked batches on kitchen paper to absorb any excess oil.

Meanwhile, combine the salt and pepper in a large bowl. Toss the cooked calamari in the sea salt flakes and black pepper, and serve immediately with lemon wedges and a very simple rocket salad.

*Serves 4*

4 medium-sized calamari tubes
115 g (4 oz/1 cup) cornflour (cornstarch)
115 g (4 oz/1 cup) plain (all-purpose) flour
Rapeseed (canola) or vegetable oil, for deep frying
Sea salt flakes
Freshly cracked black pepper
Lemon wedges and rocket (arugula) salad, to serve

# Mains

*This dish can be served hot or cold as a snack or a main meal. If you're having it as a warm main meal, serve with a side dish of your favourite vegetables or salad.*

# SACCOCCE DI MELANZANE

## BAKED AUBERGINE WITH CHEESE AND HAM

*Serves 4*

2 large aubergines
(eggplant)

500 ml (18 fl oz/2 cups)
milk

4 eggs

8 bocconcini cheeses, sliced

8 slices Italian parma ham

250 g (9 oz/2½ cups)
breadcrumbs

½ teaspoon salt

½ teaspoon pepper

Plain (all-purpose) flour,
for dusting

500 ml (17 fl oz/2 cups) oil,
for frying

To prepare the aubergine, wash, dry, then slice them lengthways into 1 cm (½ in)–thick slices. Cut 8 slices from each, discarding those from each end with the skin on. Put the sliced aubergine in a colander with a sprinkling of salt between each layer. Leave to stand for 20 minutes. Rinse, then pat each slice dry with kitchen towel.

Whisk the milk and eggs together in a large bowl until well combined. Set aside. Pour the breadcrumbs into a shallow baking tray and season with salt and pepper. Mix well and set aside.

Place 8 aubergine slices on the work surface. Arrange slices of one bocconcini on each aubergine followed by a slice of ham. Add an aubergine slice on top to create a sandwich.

Put the flour into a large shallow bowl. Dip each aubergine sandwich lightly in the flour and shake off the excess.

Soak each floured sandwich in egg wash, then turn in the breadcrumbs, patting down firmly to make sure the crumbs adhere.

Heat the oil in a large fry pan over a medium heat. Fry the 2 aubergine sandwiches for 2 minutes on each side, or until golden brown. Drain on kitchen paper. Continue to work in batches of 2 until all the aubergine sandwiches are cooked. Serve hot or cold.

*Any medium or firm-fleshed fish will work for this recipe. Chicken will also work for this dish, just vary your cooking time depending on the size and cut of your chicken. Serve with roasted chat potatoes and sautéed broccolini.*

# GRILLED (BROILED) FISH

Preheat the grill (broiler) to medium-high heat. Mix together the oil, salt flakes and black pepper in a large dish. Place each fish fillet, one at a time, in the olive oil mix and turn to coat well.

Position the fillets skin-side down on a hot grill (broiler) pan and cook for 4 minutes. Carefully turn the fish over and cook for another 4 minutes, or until cooked through. The cooking time depends on the thickness of the fillet. Top each fillet with 15 ml (1 tablespoon) of salsa verde.

*Serves 4*

60 ml (4 tablespooons) extra
   virgin olive oil
I teaspoon sea salt flakes
I teaspoon freshly cracked
   black pepper
4 firm-fleshed white fish
   (seabass, halibut or
   barramundi fillets), each
   300 g (II oz)
Lemon wedges, for serving
60 ml (4 tablespoons) Salsa
   Verde, for serving (see
   Sauces, Stocks & Dressings)

# GRILLED SEAFOOD PLATTER

2 baby seabass, halibut or
   barramundi fillets, skin off
   (flathead tails can also be used)
½ cup plain (all-purpose)
   flour, for coating
8 large tiger prawns, raw and
   shells off
8 large scallops (roe on or off)
10 scored squid (calamari)
   (see how to score calamari in
   Entreés)
6 green mussels, halved (if still
   in shell, remove shell)
4 oysters kirkpatrick
4 oysters, no prep required

MARINADE
1 tablespoon garlic, crushed
60 ml (4 tablespoons) olive oil
Salt and pepper
Parsley, finely chopped, to
   garnish

SALAD
200 g (7 oz) rocket (arugula)
   leaves
¼ Spanish (Bermuda) onion,
   sliced
150 g (5 oz) Parmesan cheese
   shavings

Coat fish in flour on a plate.

To prepare the marinade, mix all the ingredients together and marinate seafood (except for oysters kirkpatrick) for one hour minimum. Can be done overnight.

Preheat the grill (broiler) to medium heat. Put the fish on the grill (broiler) pan and cook for about 2 minutes. Turn it over, so skin side is down and cook for another 2 minutes, or until cooked through. When fish becomes flaky you know it has cooked through.

Put the remaining marinated seafood, in order of prawns, scallops, mussels, calamari, on the grill with the turned barramundi. Cook until golden brown on both sides, for about 7 minutes. Check barramundi is ready and serve all ingredients on a platter.

Use salad ingredients to garnish.

*In Italian, Saltimbocca means 'jump in the mouth', meaning a mouthful of flavour.*

# CHICKEN SALTIMBOCCA

Preheat the oven to 180°C/350°F/Gas Mark 4. To prepare the chicken, butterfly the chicken breast using a fillet knife. Starting from the narrow end of the lobe, slice halfway through the thickness of the chicken, cutting almost all the way through. Spread the breast open and you have a butterflied chicken breast. Very gently, using the flat side of a meat hammer, beat each portion to a thickness of 1 cm (½ in), then cut each portion into three pieces.

Put a piece of Brie on each piece of chicken. Cover the chicken with a slice of prosciutto.

Heat the olive oil in large ovenproof frying pan over a medium heat. Add the chicken with the Brie side face up. Fry for 5 minutes or until the underside of the chicken is lightly browned. Do not turn the poultry.

Add the wine, stock, garlic and cream to the pan, bring it to a simmer, then put the pan in the preheated oven until the sauce is reduced by half.

Remove the chicken from the pan and keep warm on a foil-wrapped plate. Return the pan with the sauce to the hob, add the butter and simmer over a medium heat until reduced to a thick sauce.

Plate up the chicken on a bed of velvety mashed potatoes and serve with sautéed baby spinach or roasted root vegetables. Pour over the sauce. Garnish with chopped parsley.

*Serves 4*

4 chicken breast portions, each 250 g (9 oz)

300 g (11 oz) Brie, cut into 12 equal pieces

12 thin slices prosciutto

50 ml (2¾ fl oz/⅓ cup) olive oil

100 ml (4½ fl oz/⅔ cup) dry white wine

750 ml (26 fl oz/3¼ cups) chicken stock

2 cloves garlic, peeled and finely chopped

250 ml (9 fl oz) pouring cream

50 g (2 oz) butter

Salt and finely ground black pepper

Fresh Italian parsley, finely chopped, to garnish

*You could also use veal for this recipe in place of the chicken, if you like. Serve with mashed potato and sautéed spinach.*

# CHICKEN SCALLOPINI

*Serves 4*

16 chicken tenderloins

100 ml (3½ fl oz) olive oil

1 teaspoon fresh sage, finely chopped

1 teaspoon fresh thyme, finely chopped

1 teaspoon fresh rosemary, finely chopped

1 teaspoon fresh parsley, finely chopped

1 teaspoon garlic, peeled and chopped

750ml (26 fl oz/3 cups) chicken stock

Juice of 2 lemons

100 g (3½ oz) butter

Salt and pepper

Preheat the oven to 200°C/400°F/Gas Mark 6. With a meat tenderiser tool, gently hammer all the tenderloins to the same thickness, about 5 mm (¼ in).

Heat a large, ovenproof heavy frying pan over a medium heat. Add half the oil and 8 tenderloins. Cook both sides until golden, about 3 minutes each side. Heat the remaining oil and cook the remaining chicken in the same way. Set aside as before.

In the same pan, gently heat the herbs with any remaining oil or juice from the chicken. Stir for 1 minute, then return the cooked chicken to the pan with the stock, lemon juice and butter. Melt the butter and stir in.

Put the pan in the oven and bake until the liquid has reduced by half. Remove the chicken from the pan, place to the side on a kitchen paper-lined plate and keep warm.

Put the pan over medium heat on the hob and bring to a simmer, stirring continuously until the sauce is reduced and thickened. Pour over the chicken and serve.

*Use the backstrap of the lamb as it's a very tender cut of meat. It comes from the top of the back of the lamb and is a muscle that isn't used often, so it remains tender. You'll need to order this cut of meat through your local butcher. You can serve this dish with any mash and vegetables.*

# HERB AND NUT-CRUSTED LAMB

To make the herb and nut coating, put the rosemary and thyme in a food processor or blender and process until very fine, about 1 minute. Add the cashew and pine nuts and blend for another 2 minutes. Add the oregano, basil and paprika and process for 30 seconds.

Add the breadcrumbs and cheese to the food processor and continue to blend for another 30 seconds. Season with salt and pepper, to taste. Pour into a large shallow dish and cover with kitchen foil to make an airtight container. Refrigerate until ready to use. Preheat the oven to 180°C/350°F/Gas Mark 4.

Whisk the egg and milk together in a small bowl until combined. Decant into a large, shallow dish.

Put the flour in a shallow dish, season with salt and pepper, and coat the lamb on all sides. Dust off any excess, then dip the floured lamb in egg wash.

Roll each piece of lamb in the herb and nut coating, pressing it firmly to ensure the coating adheres.

Heat the olive oil in a large frying pan until hot enough for frying. To test if the oil is hot enough, dip a small sample of meat into the oil and it should instantly sear if hot enough. Fry each piece of lamb for about 5 minutes on each side until browned all over. When cooked, let the lamb sit in the warm oven for 3–5 minutes, so all the juices go through the meat and it is cooked medium throughout. Then serve.

*Serves 6*

½ cup fresh rosemary, chopped
½ bunch thyme
115 g (4 oz/1 cup) cashew nuts
55 g (2 oz/½ cup) pine nuts
2 tablespoons dried oregano
2 tablespoons dried basil
2 tablespoons paprika
15 g (½ oz/¼ cup) breadcrumbs
6 tablespoons Parmesan cheese, grated
Salt and pepper
250 g (9 oz/1 cup) plain (all-purpose) flour, for dusting
1 egg
120 ml (4 fl oz/½ cup) milk
6 lamb backstraps, approx. 200 g (7 oz) per backstrap
250 ml (9 fl oz/1 cup) olive oil, for shallow frying

*Lamb shank is traditionally a tough section of meat on the shin bone of the lamb, therefore we braise it for several hours to tenderise it. I've chosen to not include tomato and red wine in this recipe to increase the sweetness and decrease the acidity, which is good for those who suffer heat burn or stomach complaints.*

# LAMB SHANKS

*Serves 4*

Extra virgin olive oil, spray only

8 lamb shanks (ask your butcher to French cut them for you)

2 medium carrots, diced into 2 cm (¾ in) cubes

2 celery stalks, sliced into 1 cm (½ in) lengths

2 medium brown onions, peeled and finely diced

5 cloves garlic, peeled and crushed

1 teaspoon fresh rosemary, finely chopped

1 cup thyme

1 teaspoon salt

750 ml (26 fl oz/3 cups) white wine

2 litres (70 fl oz/8 cups) beef stock

230 ml (generous 8 fl oz/1 cup) beef jus (see Sauces, Stocks & Dressings)

50 g (2 oz) butter

Salt and freshly ground black pepper, to taste

Preheat the oven to 200°C/400°F/Gas Mark 6. Spray a baking tray with olive oil spray. Lay shanks in the baking dish and cook in oven for 20 minutes. Remove from oven and set aside.

Meanwhile, mix cut vegetables with garlic and herbs in a mixing bowl. Transfer vegetables into the lamb shank baking tray.

Add the salt, wine and beef stock, ensuring the shanks and vegetables are completely covered. Cover the pan with foil and bake for 2 hours at 160°C/315°F/Gas Mark 2–3, turning after the first hour (keep covered). Remove the foil and turn shanks over.

Return the tray to the oven, uncovered, for another 30 minutes. Remove the shanks from the tray, cover and set aside to keep them warm.

Strain the juices and vegetables into a bowl. Discard the vegetables and return the juices to the pan. Place on the hob over high heat and add the beef jus. Bring to the boil, then reduce to a simmer and add the butter. Cook until thick and glossy. Season to taste with salt and pepper.

Serve the lamb shanks with polenta or mash and sautéed broccolini. Pour over the thickened sauce.

*Panko breadcrumbs are a Japanese breadcrumb, made from a very dry bread which has been toasted before being crumbed to remove any remaining moisture. The crumb itself is larger than the traditional breadcrumb, which gives it a crunchier texture. Serve with sweet potato mash and some sautéed greens.*

# HERB-CRUSTED LAMB CUTLETS

Preheat the oven to 150°C/300°F/Gas Mark 2. Put the flour in large bowl, season with salt and pepper and set aside.

In a large bowl, make an egg wash by whisking together the milk and eggs until well combined. Set aside.

In a baking tray, mix the freshly chopped herbs with both quantities of breadcrumbs and season with the salt and pepper.

One at a time, cover each lamb cutlet in flour and shake off any excess.

Coat each floured cutlet in egg wash, then transfer to the tray of seasoned crumb mix and press each cutlet down firmly to make the herby crumb mix adhere. Repeat to coat each cutlet.

Fill a large, heavy frying pan with oil to a depth of 3 mm (1/8 in). Heat over a medium heat then fry the cutlets in batches of three or four at a time, so that the temperature of the oil does not drop too much. Fry the cutlets for 2 minutes on each side, or until crumb coating turns golden brown. Put the cutlets in the oven for 15 minutes to keep them warm as you cook.

*Serves 5*

500 g (1¼ lb/5¼ cups) plain (all-purpose) flour, for coating

1.5 litres (52 fl oz/6 cups) milk

5 eggs

½ bunch fresh sage, finely chopped

½ bunch fresh thyme, finely chopped

½ bunch fresh oregano, finely chopped

½ bunch fresh flat leaf parsley, finely chopped

275 g (10 oz/3 cups) Panko breadcrumbs (or breadcrumbs made from fresh bread)

275 g (10 oz/3 cups) breadcrumbs (made from old bread)

2 teaspoons salt

1 teaspoon cracked black pepper

15 French-trimmed lamb cutlets

1 cup (250 ml/9 fl oz) vegetable oil, for frying

*This dish transforms an ordinary piece of meat into something with colour and extra flavour to impress those who appreciate Mediterranean tastes. Serve with your favourite vegetables.*

# STUFFED LAMB BACKSTRAP

*Serves 4*

4 lamb backstraps, each 250 g (9 oz)

8 thin slices prosciutto

8 large basil leaves

4 pieces provolone cheese, each 8 x 3 cm (3 x 1 in)

With a small, sharp knife, cut a slit in one side of each piece of lamb, effectively making a pocket and leaving 1 cm (½ in) uncut on the three remaining sides so the filling will not come out. Place your fingers in the pocket and make each a little wider so the filling will fit.

Overlap slightly two pieces of ham on a work surface. Put a basil leaf in the centre. Add a piece of cheese on top, followed by another basil leaf. Wrap the ham around the cheese and basil to make a parcel. Repeat with the remaining ham, basil and cheese pieces. Stuff once parcel in each piece of meat.

Preheat the grill (broiler) to a medium heat, and grill (broil) the lamb for 7 minutes on each side, or until cooked to your liking. This should be 7 minutes each side for rare-medium, otherwise longer if you prefer well-done.

Put the cooked lamb on a warmed plate and cover with kitchen foil for 5 minutes to rest the meat before serving.

*Pork is a very popular meat in Italy. The Italians cook it very simply, either pan-frying with butter and olive oil, barbequed or by roasting a large piece. And it's the only meat they use to make sausages. Figs are also very popular. Almost every garden I visited in Italy has a fig tree. You will also find pure honey all over Italy as many Italians keep their own bees. This dish is slightly sweet and sticky.*

# MAIALE CON FICO

## ROAST PORK WITH FIGS

Place all ingredients in a large bowl and marinate in the fridge for at least 4 hours, although overnight will enhance the flavours.

Remove pork from marinade. Heat grill plate or frying pan on medium heat. Once heated, add drained pork and cook for approximately 20 minutes, turning the meat over every 5 minutes. Cook for less or longer according to how you like your meat cooked. A cooking time of 20 minutes will cook the meat to medium.

Place cooked pork on top of the Fig and Beetroot Salad.

*Serves 6*

½ cup good-quality balsamic vinegar
1 cup extra virgin olive oil
¼ cup honey
2 tablespoon garlic, finely chopped
3 sprigs rosemary
6 pork eye fillets, approx. 200 g (7 oz) each
1 teaspoon salt
1 teaspoon cracked pepper
Fig and Beetroot Salad, to serve, see Salads

*Osso Bucco is Italian for 'bone with a hole'. It originates from a farming region in Lombard, Italy. Historically, the farmers were very poor, thus having to come up with tasty dishes using cheap cuts of meat. Best served with creamy polenta (refer to recipe in Side Dishes) and a side of salad.*

# VEAL OSSO BUCCO

*Serves 4*

12 pieces veal osso bucco

3 celery stalks, leafy tops removed and sliced

2 carrots, peeled and diced

2 brown onions, peeled and diced

3 garlic cloves, peeled and crushed

4 bay leaves

1 bunch fresh thyme

2 teaspoons salt

½ teaspoon freshly ground black pepper

750ml (26 fl oz/3 cups) dry white wine

3 litres (105 fl oz) chicken stock

Preheat the oven 180°C/350°F/Gas Mark 4. Put the veal pieces on a baking sheet and bake in the oven for 1½ hours, or until completely brown. Tip them into a large baking dish. Turn the oven temperature down to 170°C/325°F/Gas Mark 3.

Arrange the celery, carrot, onion, garlic, bay leaves and thyme around the meat. Pour over the white wine and stock, and cover with kitchen foil. Bake in the oven for 2½ hours, turning the veal pieces half way through the cooking time. To check if the veal is ready, it should be falling off the bone. If the meat isn't ready, return it to the oven, uncovered, for another 30 minutes.

Once the meat is tender, remove it from the baking dish and put aside on warmed serving plates.

Drain the vegetables from the baking juices as they are not required. Put the baking tray containing the juices over a medium heat on the hob, bring to a simmer and cook until it has reduced and thickened. Pour over the veal to serve.

*This is a traditional Italian pan-fried dish. I like to serve this veal dish with potato mash and sautéed baby spinach.*

# SCALLOPINI DI VITELLO

## ESCALOPES OF VEAL

To tenderise the meat, beat each piece gently with a meat mallet, without breaking through the meat. Lightly dust the veal with flour and set aside.

Heat a large frying pan over high heat. Add the olive oil and 125 g (4½ oz) of the butter. Working in batches, if necessary, as soon as the butter melts, add the veal to the pan and fry for one minute on each side.

Add the sliced mushrooms, garlic, salt, pepper and parsley to the pan and cook on high heat until the mushrooms are tender.

Add the wine and continue to cook on high heat for 10 seconds stirring constantly. Add the stock and the remaining butter and bring to the boil. Cook for 2 minutes. Remove the meat from the pan and keep warm. Stir the sauce continuously.

Remove the pan from the heat, return the meat to the pan and allow to rest for 1 minute before serving.

*Serves 4*

1 kg (2¼ lb) veal shoulder, sliced 1 cm (½ in) thick

Plain (all-purpose) flour, for dusting

100 ml (3½ fl oz) olive oil

175 g (6 oz) butter

400 g (14 oz) button mushrooms, washed and sliced

2 cloves garlic, peeled and finely chopped

1 teaspoon salt

1 teaspoon freshly ground black pepper

200 ml (7 fl oz) white wine

600 ml (21 fl oz/2½ cups) chicken stock

*I like to serve this dish with creamy potato mash and sautéed baby spinach.*

# VITELLO RIPIENO CON VEDURA ALLA GRIGLIA

## VEAL STUFFED WITH GRILLED VEGETABLES AND CHEESE

*Serves 4*

1 small aubergine
  (eggplant)

1 medium courgette
  (zucchini), trimmed

1 medium red (bell)
  pepper, washed,
  halved, stalk and seeds
  removed

4 veal steaks, approx.
  220 g (7–8 oz) each

100 g (3½ oz) haloumi
  cheese, cut into equal
  4 pieces

Plain (all-purpose)
  flour, for dusting

Olive oil or olive oil
  spray, for grilling
  (broiling)

250 ml (9 fl oz/1 cup)
  port

2 garlic cloves, peeled
  and crushed

100 g (3½ oz) butter

To prepare the vegetables, cut the aubergine and courgette into batons 2 x 8 cm (¾ x 3¼ in). Slice the bell pepper into 2 cm (¾ in) wide strips.

Preheat the grill (broiler), put the aubergine, courgette and pepper on the grill pan or very lightly oiled frying pan and cook for 2 minutes on each side. Set aside to cool. Preheat the oven to 200°C/400°F/Gas Mark 6.

Arrange each piece of veal on the work surface. Put equal amounts of vegetables on top of each, and top with a piece of cheese. Roll up the meat, cheese and vegetables and secure each roll with a wooden cocktail stick.

Decant the flour onto a plate and lightly roll each piece of veal in it. Shake off the excess. Over a medium heat, heat the olive oil, then lightly fry the veal for approximately 3–4 minutes until brown all over. Remove the veal from the pan, but retain the juices.

Put the veal on a baking tray and bake in the oven for 5–7 minutes, or until the cheese is slightly melted; you may see it oozing through the rolled ends of the meat. Remove from oven and keep warm.

Meanwhile, heat the pan containing the juices, add the port and garlic and bring to a simmer until all the sediment has lifted from the bottom of the pan, stirring. Add the butter and cook for 2–3 minutes, or until the sauce has reduced, and is thick and glossy.

Transfer the meat to the warmed dinner plates and pour over the port reduction.

*This dish will have your guests thinking that you've been slaving in the kitchen for hours, but little do they know it has been looking after itself. Ox cheeks are now readily available from most butchers. Check with your local butcher. Although very tasty, it is a tough meat, so lengthy cooking tenderises it.*

# BRAISED OX CHEEKS

Preheat the oven to 170°C/325°F/Gas mark 3. Heat the oil in a large ovenproof pan over a high heat and add the ox cheeks. Brown the meat all over, about 8 minutes. Remove the meat from the pan and set aside.

To the same pan, add the carrots, celery, onion, thyme and garlic. Lightly fry them over a medium heat for 1 minute then return the browned meat to the pan. Add a pinch of salt, the wine and beef stock to the pan making sure the cheeks are covered with liquid.

Cover the pan with foil or lid and bake in the preheated oven for 1 hour. Remove the foil or lid and turn the meat over. Return pan to the oven, uncovered, for another 30 minutes.

Remove the meat from the pan, setting it aside to keep warm under foil. Strain the pan juices through a sieve into a small bowl, discard the vegetables and return the strained juices to the pan.

Place over a high heat and add the beef jus. Bring the liquid to the boil, then reduce to a simmer. Add the butter and cook until thick and glossy and thickened a little, stirring continually. Season to taste.

Serve the ox cheeks with polenta or mashed potato and sautéed greens. Pour the thickened sauce over the meat and serve immediately.

*Serves 4*

100 ml (3½fl oz/½ cup) olive oil

8 small ox cheeks

2 carrots, diced into 1 cm (½ in) cubes

2 stalks celery, diced into 1 cm (½ in) cubes

2 medium brown onions, diced into 1 cm (½ in) cubes

½ bunch thyme

5 cloves garlic, peeled and crushed

salt

750 ml (26 fl oz/3 cups) red wine

2.5 L (88 fl oz/10 cups) beef stock

120 ml (4 fl oz/½ cup) beef jus

25 g (1 oz) butter

Freshly ground black pepper, to taste

# MY SUNNY-DRIED TOMATOES

*After a bumper season of tomato growing in 2009, I looked at the harvest and wondered how we were going to consume it before everything spoiled. 'Ah, sun-dried!', I thought. What a great way to conserve these sweet, fleshy, juice-filled goodies so that we will be able to enjoy them all year round.*

*Here's how I went about it. Firstly, I thought back to a conversation I overheard during my last late summer Italian holiday. Two older woman discussed, in their native tongue, how it was a better idea to preserve the fruits of their labour, by drying them under the Mediterranean sun, than feeding them to the birds.*

*Reciting the words of these wise women, I washed the tomatoes, cut them in half and laid them on sheet-covered trestle tables (cut side up so the inside flesh was exposed). Grabbing handfuls of cooking salt, I sprinkled these over the tomatoes. I left the tomatoes to rest under my sun for five days, bringing them indoors each night. Five days later, I washed the excess salt off my little gems with water and later returned them to lie under the sun for one last day of drying, to ensure they were completely dried out.*

*Using whole, peeled cloves of garlic, fresh oregano, extra virgin olive oil, capers, basil and my new sun-dried tomatoes, I layered sterile glass jars with all these ingredients till they were full (no pockets of air) and put the jars away for two months to allow the flavours to infuse and the oil to soften the tomatoes. These would be the perfect accompaniment to my homemade salami.*

# HOMEMADE SALAMI AND SAUSAGE

*My favorite food to make is pork salami because I love the robust richness and saltiness of the flavours.*

*The process begins after a full moon (traditionally, it is believed that this will ensure the meat will be of a better quality), with a family pilgrimage to a local farm where we select a couple of healthy young sows. The selected sows are then prepared by a local butcher on the farm and we collect the mince for our sausages and salami. By this stage we have approximately 200 kilograms (440 pounds) of pork mince.*

# ITALIAN SALAMI

*1 kg (2 lb 4 oz) mince makes approx. 1 long salami)*

27 g (¾ oz) salt per 1 kg
  (2 lb 4 oz) pork mince
100 ml (3½ fl oz) red wine
100 gm (3½ oz) pepperoncino
  conserve (concentrated
  pepper paste), available from
  any Italian deli
Sausage casing (available from
  your local butcher)

Knead the salt into the mince for approximately 1 minute per 1 kilogram (2 lb 4 oz).

Add in the red wine and pepperoncino conserve into salted mince and knead everything together. Cover and refrigerate overnight.

The next day, fill sausage casings and tie the ends with string to seal, ensuring no air pockets.

Hang in a smoke house for two weeks (smoking is optional).

Hang for a further four weeks in dry, cool place, rubbing each salami with white vinegar every three days (to prevent mould).

# ITALIAN SAUSAGE

Knead the salt into the mince for approximately 1 minute per 1 kg (2 lb 4 oz).

Add remaining ingredients and knead for a further minute

Fill sausage casings and tie ends with string to seal, ensuring no air pockets, for desired sausage length.

Sausages are ready to cook and eat on own or accompany with anything you like.

The best way to cook Italian sausages is on a low to medium heat in a covered fry pan. Do not add oil to the pan.

*1 kg (2 lb 4 oz) mince makes approx. 5 sausages*

25 g (¾ oz) salt per 1 kg (2 lb 4 oz) pork mince

50 g (1¾ oz) dried fennel seeds

100 ml (3½ fl oz) dry red wine

Pinch black pepper

¼ teaspoon garlic, minced

¼ teaspoon dried oregano

5 sausage casings (available from your local butcher)

Pasta

# VIC'S HOMEMADE PASTA

Place flour and salt in a bowl and make a well in the centre. Put the eggs and olive oil into the well and mix the flour into the liquid well with your index and middle fingers. Mix together till you've made a pliable dough. If you feel it's a little dry, add some water but just a little by little. Knead the dough on a floured surface for about 10 minutes until dough become elastic-like. Cover the dough in cling wrap and set aside for about 30 minutes.

Roll out pasta dough into 10 separate 'sausages' and work through your pasta machine according to its instructions to get it nice and thin. Once the pasta is about 10 cm (4 in) wide you're done.

Have a large pot of water on rapid boil, add the extra salt, and place pasta in the boiling water in two separate batches. The time it takes to cook is usually according to which pasta you have chosen to make on from machine's instructions. Regular-sized fettuccine usually take about 3 minutes to cook. Try not to overcook your pasta as it will taste gluggy. Italians like to serve their pasta 'al dente' meaning 'to the tooth'. This means when you bite into the pasta, you want to feel your teeth go slightly through it so that the pasta still feels firm but cooked.

*Serves 6–8*

1 kg (2 lb 4 oz) plain flour

Pinch salt

10 whole eggs

2 egg yolks

2 tablespoons extra virgin
  olive oil

Extra salt, for pasta

# MY NAPOLI SAUCE STORY

*I think sauce day is one of the most labour-intensive, alcohol-fuelled and stomach-indulged days of the year. Sauce day begins the night before when the family gathers together with boxes of specially hand-picked, plump and ripe tomatoes.*

*We cut the tomatoes in half and lightly sprinkle them with cooking salt—this helps reduce the water in the tomato and leave us with a richer-tasting sauce. Finally, we stack our lightly salted tomatoes in tubs with drainage holes and leave overnight.*

*Sauce day arrives—the family rises with the sun, as does the tomato squeezing machine, and the processes begin. All tomatoes go through one end of the machine, the skins are removed, and sauce flows out the other end and is caught in a huge container.*

*Fresh basil and oregano are added to the rich sauce, which is later sealed in sterile glass bottles. These bottles are boiled for approximately 20 minutes, to air-seal each bottle and enhance the longevity. For the tastiest Napoli sauce, refer to my Napoli recipe. If you want these recipes to work out well, you must use the highest quality produce.*

*This tasty tomato sauce is the base for several of recipes in this book. Enjoy it served ladled over hot pasta and add some shavings of Parmesan cheese. This sauce can be frozen in freeze-proof containers for up to three months and can be stored in an airtight container in the refrigerator for up to five days.*

# NAPOLI SAUCE

Heat the oil in large saucepan over medium heat. Add the onions and garlic and fry, until translucent.

Add the crushed tomatoes and bring to the boil. Once boiling, add the remaining ingredients. Simmer for 1 hour, stirring regularly.

*Serves 12*

100 ml (3½ fl oz) extra virgin olive oil

1 medium red onion, peeled and finely chopped

4 cloves fresh garlic, peeled and chopped

2.5 litres (88 fl oz/10 cups) canned crushed tomatoes

2 tablespoons salt

2 tablespoons sugar (granulated or caster)

2 tablespoons fresh parsley, finely chopped

1 bunch basil, leaves washed, dried and torn up

½ teaspoon white pepper powder

*I use chicken breast for this recipe but you can use chicken thigh fillets instead with the fat and skin removed. For me, Hass avocados are the best avocados for taste and are readily available throughout the year. I like to serve this sauce with penne as the pasta seems to hold the sauce well.*

# CHICKEN AVOCADO SAUCE

*Serves 4*

100 ml (3½ fl oz) olive oil

600 g (1 lb 6 oz) chicken breast or thigh fillet, diced into 3 cm (1¼ in) cubes

4 spring onions (scallions), finely sliced

16 Portabello (Swiss brown, field) mushrooms, cleaned and sliced

120 ml (4 fl oz/½ cup) white wine

1 litre (35 fl oz) single cooking cream

50 g (1¾ oz) butter

Salt and freshly ground black pepper

2 ripe avocados, cut into 2 cm (¾ in) dice

2 cloves garlic, chopped

500 g (1 lb) penne pasta, to serve

2 tablespoons flat leaf parsley, finely chopped, for garnish

Parmesan shavings, for garnish

Heat the olive oil in a frying pan over a medium heat. When the oil is hot add the chicken until browned on all sides, for approximately 2 minutes. Turn the heat down to a fast simmer.

Add the spring onions and mushrooms to the pan. Sauté the ingredients until the mushrooms are soft, about 2–3 minutes.

To deglaze the pan, remove the pan from the heat, then add the wine to the onions and mushrooms. Return the pan to the heat and turn the heat up to a high simmer. The cold liquid will lift the caramelised sediment off the bottom of the pan. Stir the liquid to combine and continue to cook until the wine has reduced by half. Add the cream and butter and season with salt and pepper to taste. Continue to cook until the sauce is the consistency of pouring custard.

Add the avocado and cook until it is hot. Serve on top of cooked, hot penne pasta or any pasta of your choice. Sprinkle with parsley and Parmesan shavings, to serve.

*I learnt this recipe when I was cooking in Perugia, Italy. I've tried many Bolognese sauces but this one's the best. It may be similar to your mum or nonna's sauces, but I change things a little! If you use all pork mince, add 1 teaspoon of fennel seeds when frying the vegetables—it gives the dish a whole new flavour. Double the quantity and make a batch for the freezer.*

# BOLOGNESE SAUCE

Put the onion, celery, carrot and garlic pieces in a food processor, and process until small chunks remain, but not so much that the vegetables become mushy.

Heat the olive oil in a large heavy pan then add the processed vegetables. Fry on low heat, until translucent, then add the beef or pork mince. Fry the meat until thoroughly browned. Stir continuously so that the meat does not stick to the pan.

Add the wine and cook on high heat for another minute. Add the crushed tomatoes and bring to the boil. Add the rest of the ingredients and lower the heat to a gentle simmer. Cook for 1 hour and 15 minutes, stirring occasionally. Serve with your favourite pasta.

*Serves 8–10*

1 large brown onion, peeled and chopped into chunks

1 large carrot, peeled and cut into 2.5 cm (1 in) lengths

1 large celery stalk, washed, leafy tops removed and cut into short lengths

4 garlic cloves, peeled and crushed

125 ml (4 fl oz/½ cup) extra virgin olive oil

1 kg (2 lb 4 oz) beef or pork mince (or a combination of the two)

235 ml (8¼ fl oz/1 cup) dry red wine

2.5 litres (88 fl oz/10 cups) canned crushed tomatoes

2 teaspoons sugar

2 teaspoons dried oregano

2 teaspoons tomato paste

2 teaspoons fresh parsley, finely chopped

Salt

*Sopressa Salami is easy to cook with and is a nice-tasting salami that releases flavours to the dish. It's readily available in any Italian delicatessen or good supermarket. Serve with penne pasta.*

# PASTA CALABRESE

*Serves 4*

600 g (1 lb 5 oz) sopressa
  salami slices
60 ml (4 tablespoons) olive oil
40 kalamata olives
1 roasted red (bell) pepper, cut
  into strips (see Side Dishes)
4 spring onions (scallions),
  trimmed and finely sliced
2 garlic cloves, peeled and
  finely chopped
120 ml (4 fl oz/½) white wine
400 ml (14 fl oz/1¾ cups)
  Napoli sauce (see Pasta)
400 ml (14 fl oz/1¾ cups)
  thickened cream
Salt and pepper
Chilli flakes, to taste
500 g (1 lb) penne pasta

Quarter each salami slice. Heat the olive oil in frying pan over high heat. Add the salami to the pan and fry for 1 minute. Add the olives, roasted pepper, spring onions and garlic to the pan, and cook for another 3 minutes on high heat.

To deglaze the sauce, add the wine to the pan until any sediment that is stuck to the base of the pan lifts off. Add the Napoli sauce and cream. Continue to cook, until sauce is a thick and creamy consistency.

Season with salt and pepper and add the chilli flakes, to taste.

*Serve this creamy sauce with gnocchi.*

# PUMPKIN SAUCE FOR GNOCCHI

Heat the butter in large heavy pan over medium heat, until melted and bubbling. Add the onion and fry until soft, but not browned, about 2 minutes.

Add the diced pumpkin to the pan and stir continuously for 5 minutes. This method brings the sugars out of the pumpkin making a sweeter sauce.

Add enough chicken stock to cover the pumpkin by 5 cm (2 in). Cook until pumpkin is tender, approximately ½ an hour.

Remove from the heat and blend with hand-held blender, or process in batches in a food processor, until a smooth and creamy consistency is achieved. Return the pan to the heat and add the parsley and cream. Continue to cook until the sauce thickens.

*Serves 4–6*

250 g (9 oz) butter

1 large white onion, peeled and roughly chopped

1 kg (2¼ lb) pumpkin, peeled and cut into 2 cm (¾ in) cubes

Salt and pepper

Chicken stock, enough to cover pumpkin by 1 cm (½ in) when in the pan

½ bunch parsley

250 ml (9 fl oz/1 cup) cream

*Serve this delicious sauce with your favourite pasta!*

# SUGO CON SAPORE

## FLAVOURSOME RAGU

*Serves 4*

50 ml (2 fl oz) olive oil

1 large brown onion, peeled and diced

1 garlic clove, peeled and chopped

1 kg (2¼ lb) minced (ground) pork

2.5 litres (88 fl oz/10 cups) canned crushed tomatoes

1 teaspoon sugar

2 tablespoons fresh parsley, finely chopped

500 g (1 lb) preferred pasta

In large heavy pan, heat the olive oil over medium heat, fry the onion and garlic for 2 minutes, or until the onion is translucent, then add the pork. Fry until the pork meat is completely browned.

Add the crushed tomatoes, sugar and parsley. Bring to the boil, reduce the heat and simmer on a very low heat until the sauce is reduced by half, stirring every 5 minutes or so to stop the sauce from sticking to the base of the pan, approximately 1 hour.

Serve the sauce over your favourite pasta.

# WAGYU BEEF AND MUSHROOM RAGU

Place onion, carrot and celery in a food processor, processing until finely chopped but not mashed.

Add olive oil to a large, heavy-based pot and fry off processed vegetables and garlic for one minute. Add the wagyu to the pot and cook on high heat until browned, this will take approximately five minutes.

Stir in red wine, then add crushed tomatoes. Add oregano and parsley. Bring to the boil then simmer on a low heat for 1 hour.

Add mushrooms, then cook for a further 30 minutes or until the sauce is thick. Season with salt and pepper according to taste. Serve with your favourite pasta and top with shaved parmesan

*Serves 4*

1 large brown onion, peeled and quartered

1 large carrot, peeled and cut into chunks

2 celery stalks

125 ml (4 fl oz) olive oil

2 cloves garlic, crushed

1 kilo (2 lb 4 oz) wagyu rump cubed into 3 cm (1 in) pieces

250 ml (9 fl oz/1 cup) dry red wine

2.5 litre (88 fl oz/10 cups) crushed tomatoes (I use the cans imported from Italy available at most supermarkets)

2 teaspoons dried oregano

2 teaspoons parsley, chopped

500 g (1 lb) swiss brown mushrooms, sliced

2 teaspoons salt

½ teaspoons white pepper

100 g (3½ oz) shaved parmesan cheese

500 g (1 lb) pasta, to serve

*Pasta*

*This is mum's favourite pasta sauce as she calls it her 'diet pasta sauce'. She uses very little pasta and lots of this sauce and feels she's eating healthy.*

# SALSA PRIMAVERA

Serves 4

30 ml (2 tbsp) olive oil

200 g (7 oz) pumpkin, peeled and diced

200 g (7 oz) mange tout (snow peas), thinly sliced

200 g (7 oz) roasted red (bell) peppers (see Side Dishes)

200 g (7 oz) button mushrooms, wiped and sliced

½ medium Spanish (red) onion, peeled and finely sliced

2 garlic cloves, peeled and crushed

200 g (7 oz) baby spinach leaves, washed and sliced

50 g (2 oz) kalamata olives

12 sun-dried tomatoes, sliced

50 ml (1¾ fl oz) white wine

500 ml (16 fl oz/2 cups) chicken stock

50 g (2 oz) unsalted butter

500 g (1 lb) fettucine pasta, cooked to packet instructions

50 g (2 oz) Parmesan cheese shavings

½ bunch flat leaf parsley, finely chopped

Heat the olive oil in large frying pan over medium heat. Add the diced pumpkin and cook for 2 minutes.

Add the mange tout, peppers, mushrooms, onion, garlic, spinach, sun-dried tomatoes, olive and parsley, reserving 2 teaspoons of the parsley for the garnish. Fry for another 5 minutes.

Add the white wine to the pan and cook on a high simmer for 2 minutes. Add the chicken stock and the butter. Allow the butter to melt, turn up the heat and bring to the boil. Reduce the heat to a high simmer and cook until the sauce has thickened and reduced to a quarter of its original volume, approximately 5 minutes. Serve ladled onto pasta with Parmesan shavings and garnished with chopped flat leaf parsley.

# Rice & Gnocchi

*Use this recipe as a base for the following risotto recipes. It can be made ahead of schedule. Follow the instructions and add any of your favourite meat or vegetables.*

# CHEAT'S RISOTTO RICE

*Serves 4*

100 ml (3½ fl oz) olive oil

1 large white onion, peeled and finely diced

400 g (14 oz/2 cups) arborio rice

100 ml (3½ fl oz) white wine

450 ml (16 fl oz/2 cups) chicken stock

50 g (2 oz) butter

Salt

In a large heavy pan, heat the oil over a medium heat, then add the diced onion. Cook until pale golden, stirring occasionally. Add the arborio rice to the pan and stir continuously, so that the rice so does not stick to the pan, for about 5 minutes.

Turn up the heat. Add the wine and stock to the rice and onion mixture and bring to the boil. Turn the heat down to medium and stir constantly. When the rice is half cooked turn the heat down to low. At this stage the rice will be slightly translucent on the edges and white in the centre. You should not be able to bite through a grain of the rice.

Continue to cook over low heat until almost all the liquid has evaporated. Stir in the butter. Tip the rice onto a baking sheet and smooth out to a very shallow layer. The rice will continue to absorb any leftover moisture. When it is cool, store in a sealed container in the refrigerator for up to 3 days.

*For those who love a seafood dish but want variety, this risotto dish is an alternative to the traditional seafood pasta.*

# SEAFOOD RISOTTO

Heat the oil in a large pan over a medium heat. Add all the seafood except for the calamari. Cook for 1½ minutes or until the seafood is half cooked and then add the calamari, garlic, salt and pepper.

Stir for 3 minutes, then add the vegetable stock, wine and rice. Bring to boil then add parsley. Reduce the heat to a simmer until the rice has almost fully absorbed all of the liquid. If you prefer your rice less cooked, add less stock, if you prefer your rice well cooked, add more stock. Add the parsley and butter and stir through until melted.

*Serves 4*

100 ml (3½ fl oz/scant ½ cup) olive oil

12 large peeled uncooked prawns (shrimp)

500 g (1¼ lb) basa fillet, diced (any firm-fleshed fish will do)

12 green lip mussels

12 large scallops

500 g (1¼ lb) calamari, sliced into 2 cm (¾ in) strips

2 cloves garlic, peeled and crushed

1 teaspoon salt

Freshly ground black pepper, to taste

1.2 L (44 fl oz/5 cups) vegetable stock

120 ml (4 fl oz/½ cup) dry white wine

600 g (1 lb 5 oz) cheat's risotto rice (see Rice & Gnocchi)

3 tablespoons fresh parsley, finely chopped

100 g (3½ oz) butter

# CHICKEN RISOTTO

Heat the oil in a large pan over medium heat. Add the chicken and cook until golden brown, then add the mushrooms, spinach, pine nuts, semi-dried tomatoes and garlic. Cook for 5 minutes then add the spinach (already added).

Add the rice along with the chicken stock and wine. Bring to the boil then simmer until the rice has absorbed almost all of the liquid. If you prefer rice less cooked add less stock, or if you prefer rice that is well cooked add more stock. Once all the liquid is almost absorbed add the butter and stir through until melted. Season with salt and pepper.

*Serves 4*

120 ml (4 fl oz/½ cup) olive oil

1 kg (2¼ lb) chicken breast, diced

1 kg (2¼ lb) button mushrooms, wiped

400 g (14 oz) baby spinach

100 g (3½ oz) pine nuts

200 g (7 oz) semi-dried tomatoes

2 cloves garlic, crushed

600 g (1½ lb) cheat's risotto rice (see Rice & Gnocchi)

1.2 L (44 fl oz/5 cups) chicken stock

120 ml (4 fl oz/½ cup) dry white wine

100 g (3½ oz) butter

1 teaspoon salt

Freshly ground black pepper

*You will need to prepare the lamb marinade ahead of time.*

# LAMB RISOTTO

*Serves 4*

1 kg (2½ lb) lamb backstrap, sliced

1 quantity Lamb Marinade
(see recipe Sauces, Stocks &
Dressings)

50 ml (2 fl oz/¼ cup) olive oil

1 Spanish (Bermuda) onion,
peeled and thinly sliced

2 cloves garlic, peeled and sliced

250 g (9 oz) semi-dried tomatoes

200 g (7 oz) kalamata olives

1.3 l (50 fl oz/5½ cups) chicken
stock

120 ml (4 fl oz/½ cup) dry red
wine

700 g (1½ lb) cheat's risotto rice
(see Rice & Gnocchi)

2 tablespoons parsley, chopped

200 g (7 oz) feta cheese,
crumbled

1 teaspoon salt

Freshly ground black pepper

Marinate the lamb following the instructions in the recipe for Lamb Marinade in Sauces, Stocks & Dressings, for at least an hour. Marinating it overnight will give you the best results.

Heat the oil in large pan, over medium heat. Add lamb and cook until golden brown, then add the onion and garlic. Cook over a high heat for 2 minutes, then add the semi-dried tomato and olives.

Add the chicken stock, wine and rice to the pan and bring to the boil. Add the parsley. Simmer until the rice has almost absorbed the liquid. Add the crumbled feta and stir through. Season with salt and pepper, to taste. Serve.

# RISOTTO WITH GOAT'S CHEESE AND PROSCIUTTO

Heat the oil in a large pan over a medium heat. Add the prosciutto and cook until golden brown.

Add the spring onions, mushrooms and garlic. Cook for 5 minutes, then add the chicken stock and rice. Bring to the boil then add the parsley. Reduce to a simmer until the rice has almost fully absorbed the liquid. If you prefer your rice less cooked, add less stock, if you prefer it well cooked, add more stock.

Stir through the crumbled goat's cheese and butter until melted. Season to taste.

*Serves 4*

100 ml (3½ fl oz) olive oil

500 g (1¼ lb) prosciutto, thinly sliced

1 bunch spring onions (scallions), thinly sliced on the diagonal

500 g (1¼ lb) field (portabello) mushrooms, thinly sliced

2 cloves garlic, finely chopped

1.3 litre (50 fl oz/5½ cups) chicken stock

700 g (1½ lb) cheat's risotto rice (see Rice & Gnocchi)

300 g (10 oz) goat's cheese, crumbled

Salt and freshly ground black pepper to taste

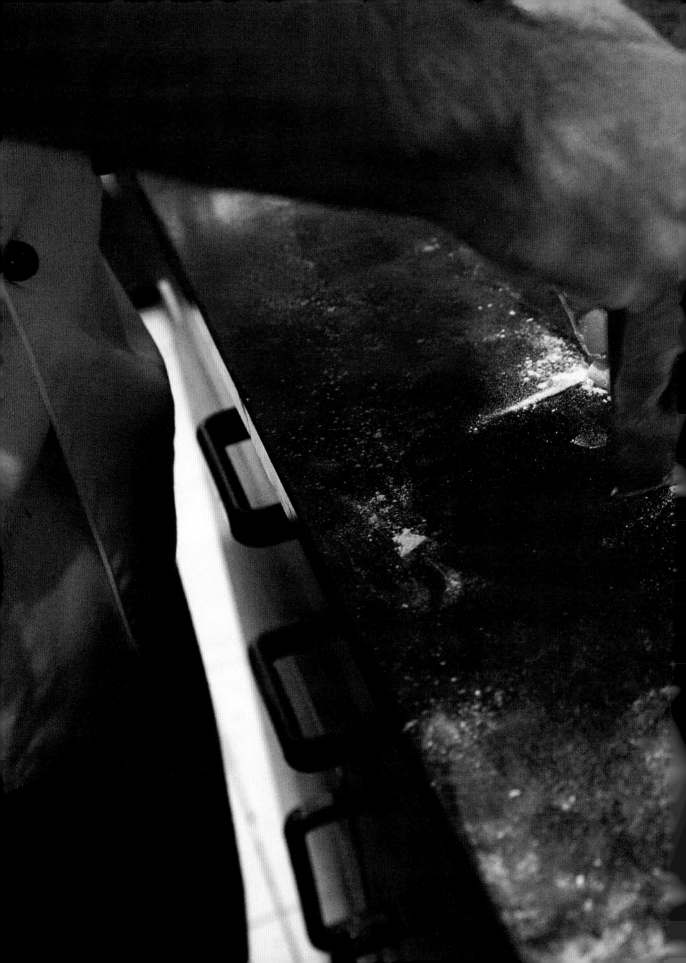

# POTATO GNOCCHI

*Serves 4–6*

1 kg (2¼ lb) desirée medium-sized potatoes, washed

400 g (14 oz/3 cups) plain (all-purpose) flour

100 g (3½ oz) butter, melted

1 egg

1 tablespoon salt

Put the potatoes (with skin on) into a large pan of salted cold water and bring to the boil. Reduce to a simmer and continue to simmer until the potatoes are tender. To test the potatoes, pierce the centre with a skewer. If it goes in easily, the potatoes are ready. Drain and set aside to cool. When cool enough to handle, remove the skins by rubbing the potatoes with your hands. Pass the skinned potatoes through a potato ricer, or mash with a potato masher until very smooth and creamy.

On a lightly floured worktop or chopping board, mix the egg and the butter together with the potato. Mix in the flour.

Knead gently until all the ingredients are just combined. Take portions of the gnocchi mixture and roll into sausages 20 cm (8 in) long and 2 cm (¾ in) diameter. Cut each into 2 cm (¾ in) lengths keeping them on a floured surface so that they don't stick to each other.

To cook the gnocchi, bring a large pan of water to the boil. Drop the gnocchi in water in batches of about 12 at a time. When they float to the surface they are ready. Remove with a slotted spoon. Serve with your favourite sauce from this book.

If you don't want to use the gnocchi immediately, you can drop the hot cooked gnocchi in iced water. Remove from water when they are cold and toss lightly with olive oil (to avoid sticking) and keep refrigerated for a couple of days. To reheat, simply drop them in boiling water for 1 or 2 minutes, just until they are hot.

# GNOCCHI GORGONZOLA

In a pot, cook the cream, cheese and chicken stock over medium heat and simmer until reduced by half.

Add cooked, warm gnocchi and butter and continue cooking over heat until thick and creamy. Once consistency is thick, season to taste and serve hot.

*Serves 4*

1 litre (36 fl oz/4 cups) cream

200 g (7 oz) gorgonzola cheese

100 ml (3½ fl oz) chicken stock

4 cups cooked potato gnocchi (see Rice & Gnocchi)

100 g (3½ oz) butter

Salt and pepper, to taste

# GNOCCHI FRITTE

*Serves 4*

500 g (1 lb) chorizo sausage, diced

2 tablespoons extra virgin olive oil

2 tomatoes, diced

2 cloves garlic, minced

4 cups cooked potato gnocchi (see Rice & Gnocchi)

¼ cup Italian flat leaf parsley, chopped

150 g (5 oz) washed rocket (arugula)

Salt and pepper, to taste

Place chorizo and oil in a large frypan and cook over medium heat until golden brown.

Turn heat to high and add tomatoes and garlic and cook for a couple of minutes.

Add warm, cooked gnocchi to pan with parsley and rocket. Once rocket is wilted, season to taste and serve.

# Side Dishes

*This dish is the perfect accompaniment with any main meal, as it incorporates a colourful and healthy variety of vegetables. The purpose of blanching is to par cook the vegetables to help maintain their true colours and flavours. This can be served with any of your favourite meat, chicken or fish dishes.*

# VEGETABLE MIX

Preheat the oven to 200°C/400°F/Gas Mark 6. Cut the carrot and parsnips into 4 cm (1½ in) slices on the diagonal.

To blanch the broccoli and French beans, put both vegetables in a pan of salted boiling water until almost tender, for 1–1½ minutes. Drain the vegetables and immediately place them into a bowl of water containing plenty of ice to cool them quickly. Drain again in colander and set aside leaving them in the colander to continue draining until they are required.

Place all the ingredients except the beans and broccoli in heatproof baking tin (pan), mix well and bake in the oven for 20 minutes. Add the broccoli to the tin, mix with the other vegetables and bake for another 10 minutes.

Add the beans to the baked vegetables and bake for another 10 minutes, or until tender.

*Serves 4–6*

1 large carrot, peeled

2 medium parsnips, peeled

1 large head broccoli, cut into 12 pieces

150 g (5 oz) fresh French (green) beans, topped and tailed

1 teaspoon salt

A bowl of cold water and ice for blanching

1 large Spanish (Bermuda) onion, peeled, halved and sliced

4 cloves garlic, peeled and crushed

125 g (4 oz) butter, melted

50 ml (1¾ fl oz) olive oil

100ml (3½ fl oz) chicken stock

½ teaspoon freshly ground black pepper

# SAUTÉED SPINACH

*Serves 2 as a side*

50 ml (2¾ fl oz/1/3 cup) olive
   oil
1 large clove garlic, peeled and
   thinly sliced
1 kg (2¼ lbs) baby spinach
salt and freshly ground black
   pepper
Juice of 1 lemon

Heat the oil in a large frying pan over a medium heat, then add garlic and fry for 1 minute.

Turn the heat up to high and add the spinach to the pan. Stir constantly until wilted. Season with salt and pepper. Serve with a sprinkle of lemon juice.

# BRAISED SWISS CHARD

Rip the silver beet leaves off the stems. Discard the white stems. You can use the stalk too, if you like.

Add 1 teaspoon of salt to a large pan of boiling water and add the Swiss chard. Cook for 2 minutes then drain and immediately place the leaves in the bowl of ice water to blanch them. When it is completely cold, drain well. This can take a few minutes as you want to get as much water out of the leaves as possible.

Heat the oil in a large frying pan or wok and add the garlic and chilli. Fry on medium heat for one minute. The garlic will taste bitter if it burns. Add the Napoli sauce to the pan and cook on high heat for 2 minutes. You want the sauce to bubble and reduce a little.

Add the drained Swiss chard to the frying pan and sauté for 10 minutes on medium heat, or until the leaves are soft. Season with salt and pepper and add lemon juice. Serve immediately.

*Serves 4–6*

1 large bunch large Swiss chard (silver beet), washed and dried

1 teaspoon salt

large bowl of ice and water

30 ml (2 tablespoons) extra virgin olive oil

2 cloves garlic, peeled and thinly sliced

Pinch of chilli flakes, or to taste

1 cup Napoli sauce (see Pasta)

Salt and pepper

Juice of 1 lemon

*Side Dishes*

*Broccolini is not unlike broccoli, but with smaller florrets and long, thin stalks. It has a mild bitterness to it. Broccoli is a fine alternative.*

# SAUTÉED BROCCOLINI

*Serves 4–6*

4 bunches broccolini, approximately 600 g (1 lb 5 oz) in total

Salt, to taste

30 ml (2 tablespoons) extra virgin olive oil

2 cloves garlic, peeled and thinly sliced

25 g (1 oz) butter

Bring a large pan of salted water to the boil. Add the broccolini, return to the boil and cook for 3 minutes or until the stalks have become tender. Drain broccolini in colander for five minutes or until all water has evaporated.

In large frying pan, heat the oil over a medium heat and fry the garlic for 1 minute. Add the broccolini to the pan and sauté for two minutes until the garlic becomes translucent. Add the butter and toss through. Serve hot.

# ROASTED RED (BELL) PEPPERS

Preheat the oven to 180°C/350°F/Gas Mark 4. Put the peppers on an ovenproof tray and bake in the oven until the skin blisters and turns black. Remove the peppers from the oven and tip into a plastic bag or bowl covered with cling wrap. Seal tightly. This will make the peppers sweat and they will be easy to peel. Leave to cool.

Peel the skin from the pepper. Cut in half and remove the seeds and any white membrane from inside. Cut into strips approximately 1 cm (½ in) wide.

Put the peppers in a bowl and add the salt, olive oil and garlic. Mix well to combine. Use immediately or place in an airtight container and refrigerate for up to seven days. If storing for later use, ensure the peppers are covered in oil at all times.

*Serves 4 as a side*

4 large red (bell) peppers
Large pinch salt
250 ml (9 fl oz/1 cup) olive oil
2 cloves garlic, peeled and
   thinly sliced

*Mum makes a few variations to this recipe by adding fresh herbs. If she is serving it with a lamb dish she'll add 1 teaspoon of chopped fresh thyme, lemon thyme or rosemary. When she serves it with a pork dish, she adds 1 teaspoon of dried basil. Experiment with any herbs you like.*

120

# CREAMY POLENTA

*Serves 4*

250 ml (9 fl oz/1 cups) chicken stock

250 g (9 oz) packet instant polenta mix

250 ml (9 fl oz) milk

½ cup Parmesan cheese, grated

50 g (1¾ oz) butter

pepper, to taste

In a very large pot, bring the stock to boil. Add the polenta mix and whisk constantly so the polenta doesn't stick to the bottom of the pot and burn. On medium heat, continue cooking while whisking it for approximately 10 minutes.

Add milk and continue whisking on medium heat for a further 5 minutes. Remove from heat and stir in the Parmesan cheese and butter and add pepper according to your taste. Allow the polenta to stand for 5–10 minutes before serving.

# SWEET POTATO MASH

*Serves 4*

1 kg (2¼ lb) sweet potato
　(kumara), peeled
200 g (7 oz) butter, at room
　temperature
¼ teaspoon freshly ground
　black pepper
Salt, to taste

Put the sweet potato in large pan with enough cold water to cover. Bring to the boil, then high simmer until the potato is just tender but retains a very slight firmness. Drain well in a colander for at least 5 minutes so all water is completely drained.

Place in food processor and process until very smooth. Remove the mash from the processor and mix in the butter and pepper. Add salt according to taste, and serve.

*My nonna was born in Treviso, Italy where polenta is a diet staple. Nonna's sisters make the best polenta. Every time I make this dish I think of them, although the authentic way is to use water rather than stock. Use polenta in place of mashed potatoes for a delicious side dish. Mum's family like to slice the cold polenta in half, fill it with salami and cheese (like making a sandwich) then grill until warmed through.*

# SET POLENTA

Pour the chicken stock into a very large pan, add the butter and bring to the boil making sure the butter has completely melted.

Stirring continuously, add the polenta in a slow trickle to the boiling stock. Keep stirring or the polenta will stick to the base of the pan and burn. Return to the boil, then reduce the heat to low. Stir constantly for about 15 minutes, or until it is thick and becoming difficult to stir.

Pour the polenta into a lightly greased baking tray and use a palate knife to smooth it to an even depth. Allow to go cold, cover with cling wrap and refrigerate for a few hours or overnight.

When the polenta is set, cut it into pieces. Under a hot grill (broiler), heat the polenta on each side until a crisp crust forms. Serve with sauce, stew or casserole.

*Serves 6–8*

500 g (1½ lb/5 cups) instant polenta
1.5 L (52 fl oz/6 cups) chicken stock
100 g (3½ oz) butter
Salt and freshly ground black pepper

*This dish could be considered too rich for some, so an alternative for the cream is skimmed milk. For those who want to celebrate the full and rich flavours, follow this recipe and enjoy it guilt-free.*

# CREAMY MASHED POTATO

*Serves 4*

2 kg (4½ lb) Desiree potatoes, peeled and quartered

1 tablespoon salt

250 g (9 oz) butter, melted

250 ml (9 fl oz/1 cup) thickened (double) cream

Salt and freshly ground black pepper

Put the potatoes in a large pan and cover with cold water and add the salt. Bring to boil, then simmer over a medium heat for 30 minutes, or until just cooked. The potatoes are cooked when you can pierce them easily with a knife. Drain well in a colander for at least five minutes or until the potatoes have dried out.

Return the potatoes to the pan and add the butter. Mash well for 1 minute, then add the cream, and salt and pepper, to taste. Continue mashing until completely smooth. If you prefer softer mash, add a little warm milk or cream. For drier mash, add less cream.

*This dish is the perfect side dish to any main meal in this cook book. I recommend you accompany it with any red meat, especially steak.*

# ROASTED CHAT POTATOES

Preheat the oven to 180°C/350°F/Gas Mark 4. Put the potatoes in a large pan of cold water with 1 teaspoon of the salt. Bring to a rapid boil and boil for 2 minutes. Drain well until all the water has evaporated and the potatoes are dry.

Spread the cooked potatoes evenly on a baking tray. Add the crushed garlic, a grinding of pepper, the oil, butter, rosemary and remaining salt and mix well with your hands to ensure the ingredients are evenly distributed.

Bake for 10 minutes. Remove from the oven, stir well, then return to the oven to bake for another 10 minutes. Repeat this step until the potatoes are golden brown all over. The time this takes will depend on the size of potatoes and whether your oven is fan-forced or not. Mix the parsley through potatoes, then serve.

*Serves 4–6*

1 kg (2¼ lbs) small chat, or baby potatoes, washed and halved

2 teaspoons salt

2 cloves garlic, peeled and crushed

fresh cracked black pepper, to taste

125 ml (4½ fl oz) olive oil

125 g (4½ oz) butter, diced

1 large sprig rosemary, leaves removed

1 tablespoon fresh parsley, finely chopped

# Salads

*This salad is a great accompaniment to pork dishes, as the sweetness of the beetroot goes perfectly with the flavours of pork.*

# FIG AND BEETROOT SALAD

*Serves 4*

2 medium fresh beetroots

30ml (2 tablespoons) honey

115ml (4 fl oz/1 cup) extra virgin olive oil

2 tablespoons garlic, finely chopped

30 ml (2 tablespoons) balsamic vinegar

½ teaspoon salt

½ teaspoon freshly cracked black pepper

8 large fresh figs, quartered

2 small red (Bermuda) onions, peeled and quartered

Cut each beetroot into eight equal pieces and boil until tender.

In a large bowl, whisk the honey, olive oil, garlic and vinegar together. Season with salt and pepper.

Place the beetroot, figs and onion into the bowl with the dressing and mix well to combine. Cover with cling wrap and marinate for at least 4 hours. Preheat the oven to 180°/350°F/Gas Mark 4.

Place all the ingredients on a baking tray and bake for 20 minutes, or until the vegetables are cooked through—do not overcook or the individual flavours of each vegetable will be lost. Serve warm or cold, with the Roast Pork with Figs dish on page 53.

*We've only put this salad on the menu and it's been a great success. I love the challenge of changing traditional recipes.*

# SALMON CAESAR SALAD

Preheat the oven to 160°C/315°F/Gas Mark 2–3. Cut each slice of bread into 2 cm (¾ in) cubes and place on a lightly greased baking tray. Bake until the bread starts to turn golden brown. Set aside to cool.

Meanwhile, preheat the grill (broiler) to a medium heat. Slice the bacon in half lengthways and grill (broil) until just crisp, or longer if you prefer it crunchy. Set aside to cool.

Wash the lettuce and pat it dry on a clean dish towel. Roughly chop the lettuce but not so finely that the leaves are too small. Place lettuce leaves in large bowl and pour over half the Caesar dressing and mix well. Divide dressed lettuce into four serving plates.

Fry or grill the salmon fillets for 3 minutes on each side. This will not cook the salmon right through, so it will not dry out. Keep the salmon warm.

Sprinkle croutons over lettuce then place poached egg on top. Now sprinkle over the shaved parmesan. Put the remainder of the Caesar dressing in squeeze bottle and squeeze evenly over each salad. Place two pieces of grilled bacon on top of each plate and top with cooked salmon.

You can add capers and/or anchovies to this recipe if you like.

*Serves 2*

4 slices ciabatta, pane di casa
  or other good quality bread
oil, for greasing
4 rashers (strips) bacon
2 small Cos lettuce
4 salmon fillets, each 150 g
  (5 oz)
200 g (7 oz) freshly shaved
  Parmesan cheese
4 poached eggs
400 ml (13 fl oz/1½ cups)
  Vic's Caesar Dressing (see
  Sauces, Stocks & Dressings)

# GARDEN SALAD

*Serves 4*

½ cos, butter or iceberg
  lettuce with the darker outer
  leaves removed

2 firm ripe tomatoes, washed,
  dried and quartered

½ medium-sized red
  (Bermuda) onion, thinly
  peeled and sliced

2 small Lebanese cucumbers or
  ½ continental cucumber,
  skin removed

90 ml (3 fl oz) balsamic
  vinaigrette (see Sauces,
  Stocks and Dressings)

Salt and pepper, according to
  taste

Wash and dry lettuce leaves. Break each leaf into bite-sized pieces.

In a large bowl, add all the vegetables and toss well. Once all vegetables are mixed, add vinaigrette, salt and pepper and toss well.

Serve as a side dish with many main meals.

*Marinate the lamb the night before to ensure the flavours come through the meat.*
*This will make all the difference and ensure the salad tastes delicious.*

# MARINATED LAMB SALAD

Mix the lamb and the marinade together until well combined, and refrigerate overnight in a non-metallic container.

Wash and dry the baby spinach and put in a large bowl. Add the tomato, cucumber slices, onion and vinaigrette and toss well.

Heat a hot grill (broiler), griddle or frying pan, and grill (broil) the lamb for 2 minutes on each side for medium rare meat, or 5 minutes for well done.

Divide the salad between four plates. Scatter the Feta cheese over and top with cooked lamb.

*Serves 4*

1 kg (2¼ lbs) lamb backstrap (fat and sinew removed) cut into thin slices

1 quantity Lamb Marinade (see Sauces, Stocks & Dressings)

1 packet baby spinach

2 medium tomatoes, each cut into eight

1 continental cucmber, sliced

1 medium Spanish (Bermuda) onion, thinly sliced

1 quantity White Wine Vinaigrette (see Sauces, Stocks & Dressings)

200 g (7 oz) Feta cheese, cut into 2 cm (¾ in) cubes

# Desserts

*After trying many crêpe recipes I found this one to be quite foolproof. Easy for anyone to make, no matter how competent you are in the kitchen.*

# VIC'S CRÊPES

*Serves 6–8*

3 eggs
4 cups (1 litre/36 fl oz) milk
2 cups flour
Pinch salt
Non-stick cooking spray

Whisk eggs and milk until both are combined—avoid creating too many air bubbles. Once combined, add flour and mix until you create a smooth consistency. Strain mixture through a sieve to remove any lumps.

Spray a crêpe pan or a flat non-stick pan with non-stick cooking spray and put pan on burner on medium to high heat. Once pan is hot, pour 60 ml (2 oz/¼ cup) of the mixture onto the pan. After approximately one minute, or when the crêpe begins to brown on the underside, flip the crêpe over using a spatula. Cook second side for approximately 30 seconds or until lightly browned on underside and remove from pan. Continue until mixture is finished.

Cooked crêpes may be kept refrigerated in an airtight container or on a plate covered with cling wrap for up to five days. Serve with Banana and Baileys or Strawberry Sauce (refer to recipes) or with any fruits or toppings you like—one of my favourites is freshly squeezed lemon juice and sugar.

# BANANA AND BAILEYS CRÊPES WITH BRANDY CARAMEL SAUCE

To make the sauce, melt the butter and sugar in a frying pan over a medium heat until the sugar caramelises. Standing well back, add the brandy to the pan to flambé. The liquid will burst into flames for about 10 seconds.

When the flames have stopped, add the cream to the pan and bring to a rapid boil over a high heat. One the sauce is boiling, turn the heat to medium and add the banana slices. Simmer for 5 minutes.

Scoop the bananas out of the pan and divide between warmed crêpes. Continue to stir the sauce over the heat until it has a thick and creamy consistency. Pour over the bananas and crêpes. Serve with vanilla ice-cream. Garnish with a sprig of mint.

*Serves 4*

200 g (7 oz) butter
400 g (14 oz) caster (superfine) sugar
60 ml (4 tablespoons) brandy
800 ml (28 fl oz) double cream
4 large bananas, sliced
8 crêpes, to serve (see Desserts)
60 ml (4 tablespoons) Baileys liqueur
Vanilla ice cream, to serve
Mint sprigs, to decorate

# STRAWBERRY CRÊPES

*Serves 4*

500 ml (17 fl oz/2 cups) dry
   red wine
1 cup caster (superfine) sugar
2 punnet strawberries cut in
   halves
8 crêpes, to serve (see Desserts)
Vanilla ice cream, or cream, to
   serve
Mint sprigs, to decorate

Place the red wine and sugar in a pan over a high heat and bring to a rapid boil, stirring occasionally to ensure the sugar has melted. Moisten a pastry brush to brush off any sugar that caramelises on the edges of the pan. Keep over a high heat until the quantity is reduced by half, about 1½ minutes.

Add the strawberries and continue cooking over a high heat until the liquid thickens, about 1½ minutes.

Pour the mixture over the crêpes and finish your dish with cream or your favourite vanilla ice-cream. Garnish with a sprig of fresh mint.

# MOIST PINEAPPLE CUPCAKES

Non-stick cooking spray
  (cake release spray)
120 g (4 oz) caster (superfine)
  sugar
60 g (2 oz) self-raising
  (self-rising) flour
65 g (2¼ oz) plain
  (all-purpose) flour
2 large eggs
125 g (4 oz) butter, melted
1 large pineapple, peeled, core
  removed and diced
5 ml (1 teaspoon) vanilla
  extract
1 teaspoon cinnamon
1 teaspoon bicarbonate of soda
  (baking soda)

Preheat the oven to 180°C/350°F/Gas Mark 4. Lightly spray a 12-hole muffin tin (pan) with non-stick cooking spray. In a large bowl, add all the ingredients together and mix until combined.

Divide the mixture evenly between a 12-cake muffin tin. Bake for 20 minutes, or until golden brown.

*There is an abundance of fresh berries in Italy. The Italians usually just eat them fresh, but they are also delicious in this popular very light mousse-like Italian cheesecake. Substitute the berries with pineapple, if you like.*

# BERRY CHEESECAKE

Put the berries in a pan over a medium heat. Bring to the boil and stew the berries until soft. Set aside to cool.

Dissolve the gelatine in 60ml (¼ cup) boiling water and set aside.

Process the amaretto and digestive biscuits in food processor until they are fine crumbs. Decant the crumbs into a large mixing bowl and add the crushed almonds, then the melted butter, and mix well until combined. Grease and line a 25 cm (10in) springform cake tin (pan) and press the crumb mixture into the base of the tin using the back of a spoon. Put in refrigerator to set.

Put the cheeses in a large mixing bowl and beat with an electric mixer until smooth. Add the sugar, lemon juice, and stewed berries. Beat lightly until all the ingredients are combined.

With a large metal spoon, fold half of the whipped cream into the cheese and berry mixture being careful to keep in as much air as possible, then fold in the rest of the whipped cream and melted gelatine making sure the mixture is very well combined. Pour the mix onto the prepared crumb base and refrigerate overnight.

*Serves 8–10*

250 g (9 oz) fresh, frozen or tinned strawberries

250 g (9 oz) fresh, frozen or tinned raspberries

2 teaspoons powdered gelatine

125 g (4¼ oz) amaretto biscuits

125 g (4¼ oz) digestive biscuits (graham crackers)

250 g (9 oz) butter, melted

50 g (2 oz) slivered almonds, roasted and lightly crushed

250 g (9 oz) mascarpone cheese, at room temperature

250 g (9 oz) smooth ricotta cheese, at room temperature

250 g (9 oz) cream cheese, at room temperature

400 g (14 oz/2 cups) caster (superfine) sugar

15 ml (1 tablespoon) lemon juice

350ml (12 fl oz/1½ cups) whipped cream

*Growing up on a property with chicken and lemon trees, I was fortunate enough to have a never-ending supply of eggs and lemons. This is how I came up with this recipe of a rich and tangy, yet light, lemon tart.*

148

# LEMON TART

*Serves 12*

Non-stick vegetable oil spray
  (cake release spray)
400 g (14 oz) Marie or other
  plain biscuits
25 g (1 oz) caster (superfine)
  sugar
250 g (10 oz) butter, melted

FOR THE LEMON CURD FILLING
12 whole eggs plus extra egg
  yolk
25 g (1 oz) caster (superfine)
  sugar
1 tablespoon cornflour
  (cornstarch)
Rind of 2 lemons, finely grated
550 ml (19 fl oz/2⅓ cups)
  lemon juice
375 g (13 oz) butter, diced
3 cups caster (superfine) sugar,
Icing (confectioners') sugar,
  to decorate

Lightly spray a deep 30 cm (12 in) loose-base flan tin (pan) with oil. Process the Marie biscuits to a fine crumb in a food processor or blender.

In a large bowl, combine the biscuit crumbs with the sugar and melted butter. Press into the base and up the sides of the prepared baking tin, using the back of a spoon. Refrigerate for at least 1 hour.

To make the filling, whisk the eggs, sugar and cornflour together in a large heatproof bowl until completely combined. Add the lemon rind and juice to the bowl and continue to whisk until combined.

Put the bowl over a pan of simmering water without allowing the base of the bowl to contact the water. Cook, stirring constantly with a wooden spoon until the mixture has a thick custard-like consistency, about 30 minutes. Do not allow the water to boil.

Remove the bowl from the heat and whisk in the butter. Pour the lemon curd mixture into the tart case. Cover with cling wrap and refrigerate overnight. Dust with icing sugar to serve.

*If you feel like being decadent, this is the ultimate dessert for every chocolate lover. This recipe was inspired by my sister-in-law Ulrika. I loved her version of a chocolate cake so much I snuck myself an extra slice out of the refrigerator, heated it in the microwave and discovered how perfect warm torte goes with my chocolate fudge sauce.*

# HOT CHOCOLATE TORTE WITH CHOCOLATE FUDGE SAUCE

Preheat the oven to 170°C/325°F/Gas Mark 3. Grease and line a 25 cm (10 in) springform tin (pan).

Combine the flour and bicarbonate of soda in a large bowl and set aside.

Put the sugar, chocolate and butter in a heatproof bowl set over a pan of simmering water. Do not allow the base of the bowl to contact the water. Stir the mixture with a wooden spoon while it melts.

When the mixture is melted, pour it into the flour mixture and add the eggs. Stir until smooth.

Tip mixture into the prepared tin and bake for 15–20 minutes or until it doesn't spring back when touched. Allow to cool for approximately 1 hour.

Pour over the Chocolate Fudge Sauce and serve with vanilla ice cream.

*Serves 12*

400 g (14 oz) self-raising (self-rising) flour

¼ teaspoon bicarbonate of soda (baking soda)

200 g (7 oz/1 cup) caster (superfine) sugar

300 g (10 oz) dark (bittersweet) chocolate

300 g (10 oz) butter

5 eggs

Chocolate Fudge Sauce (see Desserts)

Vanilla ice cream, to serve

# CHOCOLATE FUDGE SAUCE

400 g (14 oz) dark
   (bittersweet) chocolate, max.
   70% cocoa, broken into
   small pieces
400 g (14 oz) butter
2 x 400 g (14 oz) cans
   (sweetened) condensed milk

To make the sauce, put the chocolate and butter in a large heatproof bowl set over a saucepan of simmering water. Do not allow the bottom of the bowl to come into contact with the water. Stir the mixture continuously with a wooden spoon while it melts.

After it has melted, add the condensed milk and stir briskly until combined.

*A good panna cotta should have a wobble like a not-too-firm jelly. It should not be gelatinous or runny.*

# PANNA COTTA WITH BALSAMIC AND MINT STRAWBERRIES

Spray the insides of 6 dariole moulds with non-stick cooking spray. Cut the vanilla pods in half lengthways and scrape out the seeds with a knife blade.

To make the panna cotta, put the cream, vanilla extract and vanilla seeds and simmer for 5 minutes not allowing the mixture to boil. Remove from heat.

Soak the gelatine sheets in cold water, following the instructions on the packet, until all sheets are soft. Remove the excess water from the gelatine and add them to the cream mixture stirring with a wooden spoon for approximately 1 minute or until sheets are completely dissolved.

Pour the mixture evenly into the dariole moulds, allow to cool, then refrigerate for 4 hours, or until set.

When the panna cotta is set, place you fingers gently on top of it pulling it gently away from the sides of the mould. Turn the mould out on to a plate and serve with balsamic and mint strawberries.

*Serves 6*

2 vanilla pods (beans), seeds removed

700 ml (24 fl oz) thickened cream

2.5 ml (½ teaspoon) vanilla extract

185 g (6 oz/¾ cups) caster (superfine) sugar

4 gelatine sheets

Non-stick cooking spray (cake release spray)

Balsamic and Mint Strawberries (see Desserts)

# BALSAMIC AND MINT STRAWBERRIES

*Serves 6*

2 x 250 g (9 oz) punnets fresh
   strawberries

80 g (2½ oz /⅓ cup) caster
   (superfine) sugar

50 ml (2¾ fl oz/⅓ cup)
   balsamic vinegar

6 large fresh mint leaves, cut
   into julienne strips

Hull, wash, and dry the strawberries. Cut into quarters or halve them if they are small. Put into a non-metallic bowl.

In a small saucepan heat the caster sugar and balsamic vinegar over a gentle heat, just enough to melt the sugar. Set aside until cool.

Add the mint leaves to the strawberries and stir the balsamic sauce through. Refrigerate until required.

*Four layers of cream and coffee bliss—enjoy.*

# TIRAMISU

In a large bowl, cream the eggs and the sugar using an electric mixer.

In another bowl, whip the cream until soft peaks form. Fold in the egg and sugar mixture. Add the vanilla extract, marsala and mascarpone cheese, mixing well with a metal spoon. Set aside.

In a large bowl, mix the coffee, brandy, Baileys and the extra sugar together, mixing until well combined. Dip the sponge fingers into the coffee mix for a few seconds so that they absorb as much liquid as possible. Crumble the wet sponge fingers into another bowl.

Using 4–6 brandy balloon or martini glasses, begin layering the tiramisu with a crumbled layer of sponge fingers, then adding a layer of cream mixture. Repeat until you have four layers, finishing with a cream layer.

Sprinkle the top with drinking chocolate or milo. Allow to set in the refrigerator for a few hours before serving.

*Serves 4–6*

4 egg yolks

200 g (7 oz/1 cup) caster (superfine) sugar

500 ml (17 fl oz) double cream

15 ml (1 tablespoon) vanilla extract

100 ml (3½ fl oz) marsala wine

250 g (8 oz) mascarpone cheese

500 ml (17 fl oz/2 cups) espresso coffee

30 ml (2 tablespoons) brandy

30 ml (2 tablespoons) Baileys liqueur

15 g (½ oz) caster (superfine) sugar

400 g (14 oz) sponge finger biscuits (Savoiardi)

Drinking chocolate, for dusting

*This recipe can be cooked ahead of time. The sauce will keep in the refrigerator for seven days, the figs will keep for two to three days.*

# POACHED FIGS

*Serves 6–8*

1 litre (36 fl oz) red wine

3 cups sugar

4 cinnamon sticks

2 kg (4 lb 8 oz) fresh figs

Vanilla ice cream or

    mascarpone cheese, to serve

Place all ingredients in large pan and bring to the boil. Turn the heat down to a simmer and add the figs. Simmer the figs for 10 minutes, then remove from the sauce and set aside.

Continue to simmer the sauce until it reduces to a thick and glossy consistency.

To serve, heat the sauce and figs together until very warm. Serve with vanilla ice cream or a dollop of mascarpone cheese.

*My great-aunty Paula gave this recipe to my nonna who changed the recipe slightly to suit her taste. Every celebratory gathering our family had, my nonna would make this cake. Nonna passed the recipe on to my mum who then passed it on to me. The recipe was once again changed to suit my palate and became a hit at the restaurant. It's great to eat slightly warmed or cold straight from the fridge.*

# TORTA DI RICOTTA

*Serves 10–12*

6 eggs

600 g (1lb 5 oz/3 cups) caster (superfine) sugar

225 g (8 oz) butter, melted

Grated rind of 1 lemon

5 ml (1 teaspoon) vanilla extract

50 ml (3 tablespoons) Amaretto

600 g (1 lb 5 oz/4 cups) self-raising (self-rising) flour

2 x 250 g (9 oz) tubs ricotta cheese

Non-stick cooking spray (cake release spray)

Preheat the oven to 180°C/350°F/Gas 4. Spray a 25 cm (10 in) bundt tin with non-stick cooking spray.

In a large bowl, beat the eggs and sugar together using an electric mixer until the butter turns pale in colour and all the sugar has dissolved.

Add the melted butter, lemon rind, vanilla extract and amaretto. Beat until well combined. Add the flour and beat for 1 minute, then the ricotta and beat for another minute.

Pour the batter into the bundt tin and bake for 50 minutes to 1 hour. The ricotta cake is ready when light golden brown and when a skewer inserted in the centre comes out clean.

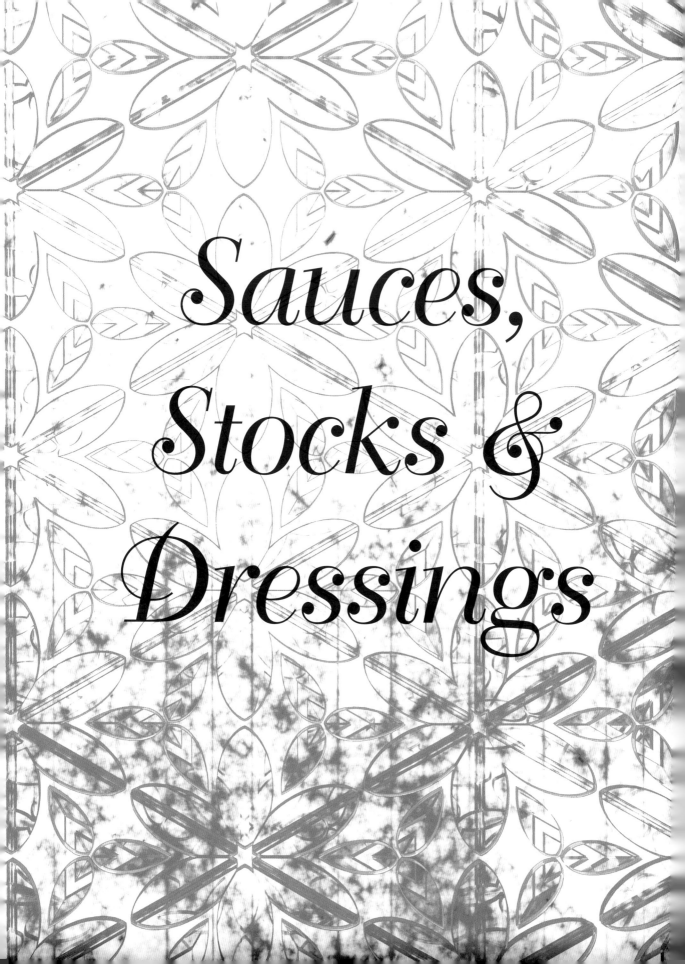

# Sauces, Stocks & Dressings

*My parents have two amazingly productive cherry trees at their home and usually enough fruit to generously give plenty away to family and friends. One year we had a glut and so I came up with this recipe to make best use of the surplus. Serve with any roasted poultry dish.*

# CHERRY CHUTNEY

Heat the oil in a medium saucepan on high heat, then add the chopped onion and cook for 5 minutes, or until the onion is translucent.

Add the pitted cherries, cider vinegar, water, Marsala wine, mustard and salt and pepper to the pan and bring to the boil. Reduce the heat to a simmer and cook for 15 minutes, or until the chutney has thickened.

Serve with roast chicken, cooked ham or roast pork. Can be served warm or cold. Preferably warm. Will keep in an air-tight container for up to two weeks.

*Serves 10–12*

30 ml (2 tablespoons) olive oil

2 red (Bermuda) onions, peeled and finely chopped

450 g (1 lb/3 cups) cherries pitted

355 ml (12½ fl oz/1½ cups) cider vinegar

355 ml (12½ fl oz/1½ cups) water

120 ml (4 fl oz/½ cup) Marsala wine

2 teaspoons mustard powder

Salt and finely ground black pepper, to taste

*Salsa Verde is a great accompaniment to any grilled fish, especially with an oily fish, as the freshness from the herbs cuts through the oiliness of the fish. It's also a very aromatic sauce.*

# SALSA VERDE

*Serves 6–8*

½ bunch basil

½ bunch parsley

400 ml (14 fl oz/generous
   1½ cups) olive oil

Juice of 1 lemon

4 anchovy fillets

1 tablespoon capers

Salt and freshly ground black
   pepper, to taste

Place all the ingredients except the salt and pepper in a food processor and pulse for two minutes until the mixture has a pesto-like consistency.

Season to taste, being careful not to add too much salt as the anchovies and capers are already salty.

# GREEN MANGO
# AND TOMATO SALSA

Mix all ingredients, except sugar and Tabasco sauce, together in a bowl. Add the sugar to balance the flavours. Spoon over freshly shucked natural oysters along with a dash of Tabasco sauce on each oyster.

*Serves 2*

1 medium green mango, peeled and finely diced

½ medium Spanish (Bermuda) onion, finely diced

1 tomato, deseeded and finely diced

Splash lemon juice

1 tablespoon parsley, finely chopped

Pinch salt and pepper

splash of vegetable oil

½ teaspoon caster (superfine) sugar

Tabasco sauce, to taste

12 oysters, to serve

*This recipe for balsamic vinaigrette can be stored in an airtight container in the fridge for two weeks. It goes well with rocket (arugula) salad.*

# BALSAMIC VINAIGRETTE

*Makes 500 ml (17 fl oz)*
150ml (5 fl oz) good-quality
  balsamic vinegar
350ml (12 fl oz) cold-pressed
  extra virgin olive oil
Salt and pepper to taste

Using a whisk, mix all ingredients together until well combined. Adjust salt and pepper according to taste.

*The most popular sauce to enjoy with any fish and can also be enjoyed with crumbed oysters. Rather than buying it off the shelf, enjoy this freshly made version, preservative free!*

# TARTARE SAUCE

Finely dice the gherkins and the capers and put in a bowl.

Pour on the Caesar dressing and stir well to combine.

Keep the sauce in an air-tight container in the refrigerator for up to two weeks.

*Makes 1 litre (36 fl oz)*
200 g (7 oz) gherkins
200 g (7 oz) capers
900 ml (32 fl oz/3¾ cups)
Vic's Caesar Dressing (see
Sauces, Stocks & Dressings)

*I've been brought up to enjoy and prepare fresh food from scratch. Mum always made her own salad dressings, so I've followed her traditions and appreciate the fresh flavours and knowing what ingredients are found within.*

174

# VIC'S CAESAR DRESSING

*Makes 500 ml (17 fl oz)*

2 egg yolks

50 ml (1¾ fl oz) white wine
  vinegar

20 ml (4 teaspoons) freshly
  squeezed lemon juice

7.5 ml (½ tablespoon) Dijon
  mustard

1 teaspoon salt

1 teapsoon powdered white
  pepper

400 ml (14 fl oz) vegetable oil

In a food processor blend the egg yolks with the vinegar, lemon juice, mustard, and salt and pepper.

Once all ingredients are combined, while the processor is still running, very slowly add the vegetable oil in a continuous fine stream. If you add the oil too fast the dressing will split and be inedible. Stop processing as soon as all the oil has been added. Serve with Caesar salad.

Store the dressing in an airtight container in refrigerator for up to two weeks.

*This vinaigrette is great for any leafy green and summer vegetable salads.*

# WHITE WINE VINAIGRETTE

Pour the vinegar, lemon juice, oregano and garlic into a large bowl. Whisk together until well combined.

Add the olive oil and season with salt and pepper to taste. Whisk for another 30 seconds. Serve with a garden or leafy green salad.

Store in airtight container in the refrigerator for up to two weeks.

*Makes 500 ml (17 fl oz)*

150 ml (5 fl oz) white wine vinegar

150 ml (5 fl oz) lemon juice

½ tablespoon dried oregano

½ teaspoon garlic, peeled and finely chopped

150 ml (5 fl oz) extra virgin olive oil

Salt and finely ground black pepper, to taste

*This marinade will be enough for 1 kilogram (2 lb 4 oz) of lamb.*

# LAMB MARINADE

*Serves 4*

50 g (1¾ oz) dried basil

50 g (1¾ oz) fresh oregano,
leaves stripped off stems

50 g (2 oz) smoked paprika

200 ml (7 fl oz) extra virgin
olive oil

2 teaspoon salt

1 teaspoon freshly ground
black pepper

90 ml (6 tablespoons) dry red
wine

60 ml (4 tablespoons) balsamic
vinegar

Mix all the ingredients together in a small bowl
and beat with a whisk.

Refrigerate until ready to use. Keep refrigerated
in airtight container for up to 2 weeks.

# MARSALA WINE SAUCE

Put the Marsala in a saucepan and bring to the boil—stand back as the Marsala will ignite. Boil for one minute, then add the remaining ingredients.

Bring the mixture back to the boil, reduce to a simmer and stir continuously until thick and it can coat the back of your spoon. You should get a gravy-like consistency. Serve immediately with your favourite fried, grilled, roasted or barbecued meats.

*Serves 4–6*
235 ml (8¼ fl oz/1 cup)
  Marsala wine
100 g (3½ oz) butter
235 ml (8¼ fl oz /1 cup)
  chicken stock
50 g (1¾ fl oz) beef jus (see
  Sauces, Stocks & Dressings)

*We use this sauce in the restaurant often. It tastes great served with plain fried, grilled or baked fish, especially the oiler types.*

# LEMON AND LIME SAUCE

*Serves 6–8*

750 ml (25 fl oz/generous 3 cups) dry white wine

1 small white onion, peeled and roughly chopped

Juice of 2 lemons

Juice of 5 limes

5 whole black peppercorns

2 bay leaves

½ tsp dried thyme

250 ml (8 fl oz) double cream

125 g (4 oz) butter

250 g (9 oz) butter

½ tsp caster (superfine) sugar

Salt and freshly ground black pepper

Put the wine, onion, lemon and lime juices, peppercorns, bay leaves and thyme in a large pan and bring to the boil. Reduce the heat to a high simmer and cook until the liquid has reduced by half, about half an hour, stirring occasionally. Strain the liquid into a clean pan, making sure you remove all traces of the herbs and vegetables.

Add the cream, butter and sugar. Cook on high simmer until the liquid is reduced by half, and the sauce is the consistency of pouring cream—it should coat the back of a wooden spoon. Add salt and pepper to taste, and serve.

*A good stock is the soul of good risotto, soup, sauce and more. You will need a large pan for stocks. I use a 12-litre (3 gallon pan). You can freeze stocks for up to six months. This recipe has been passed down from my nonna, to my mother and now to me.*

# CHICKEN STOCK

*Makes approximately 6 litres (210 fl zo)*

9 litres (2 gallons) cold water
1 large chicken, preferably free range
½ large head of celery, scrubbed, and cut into 10 cm (4 in) lengths
2 very large brown onions, peeled and quartered
3 very large carrots, peeled and cut in half lengthwise, then into 8 cm (3¼ in) lengths
½ bunch parsley stalks, cut in half
2 bay leaves
4 thyme stalks

Put the cold water into the stockpot or large pan with the chicken and bring to the boil. Turn the heat down to a simmer and remove any scum that forms on the surface. This may take a few minutes. (It is not absolutely necessary to remove the scum, but it makes clearer stock.)

Add all the vegetables and herbs and bring to the boil, then turn the heat down to a medium simmer. Place a lid ajar on the pot and cook for approximately three hours.

Remove the vegetables and chicken from the stock, strain into a bowl, leave to go cold and refrigerate it overnight. Discard the vegetables. Use the cooled chicken to make up patties, soups, sauces and sandwiches.

The following day remove the fat that has solidified on top of the stock. Freeze the stock in portions and use as required.

*Use this stock as the base of any vegetarian recipe.*

# VEGETABLE STOCK

Place all peeled and chopped ingredients in a large pan or stockpot. Bring to boil over a high heat, then turn the heat down low and simmer for 2 hours.

The following day remove the fat that has solidified on top of the stock. Freeze the stock in portions and use as required.

*Makes approx. 8 litres (17 fl oz)*

10 litres (2¼ gallons) water

5 large carrots, peeled and chopped into 5 cm (2 in) chunks

1 large head of celery, leaves removed, chopped into 5 cm (2 in) chunks

3 large white onions, peeled and chopped into chunks

2 bunches parsley stalks, no leaves

*I have learnt a couple of beef jus recipes during my career, but after a few trials, I have come up with this recipe so you, the reader can enjoy restaurant-style sauces. I have never given this recipe out and not many chefs would. So do take the time to make it, it will be well worth the effort. You will need two large baking trays, a strainer and a pot (about 30 litres/63 ½ pints), for this recipe.*

# BEEF JUS

Preheat oven to 220°C/420°F/Gas Mark 7. Place bones in baking tray. Mix tomato paste with a little water to make a runny consistency and add to bones. Roast bones in the oven for 20 minutes, or long enough to cook any meat left on the bones.

Place vegetables in another baking tray and cook in oven for approximately 15 minutes or until golden brown. Be careful not to burn.

Remove bones and vegetables from oven and place vegetables in large pot first then bones on top of the vegetables. Fill pot with cold water and bring to a simmer. You will need to remove scum from surface of stock several times. Simmer until liquid has reduced by half. This can take many, many hours.

Using a large strainer, drain the liquid from the bones and vegetables and place liquid in appropriate sized pot. Add wine to liquid and cook on low simmer to reduce the liquid by 80 per cent or until it coats the back of a wooden spoon. You now have your own beef jus ready to serve with meat or to add to many sauces to enhance flavours.

To store, wait until jus has cooled completely and place in container with cling wrap touching the top of jus, so it does not form a skin. Jus can be kept in the fridge for five or so days, or longer in the freezer.

Leftover jus can be stored in an airtight container in the fridge or freezer.

*Serves up to 20*

7 kg (15 lb ½ oz) beef bones

3 carrots, roughly chopped

3 medium brown onions, roughly chopped

4 stalks celery, cut in 4 cm (1½ in) slices

2 tablespoons good-quality tomato paste

2 x 750ml (26 fl oz) bottle dry red wine

*Egg wash is used before crumbing schnitzels, oysters, etc.*

# EGG WASH

*1 quantity*
2 eggs
240 ml (8 fl oz/1 cup) of milk

Whisk the eggs and milk together in a small bowl until well combined.

*Used to crumb meat, chicken, fish, oysters.*

# SEASONED CRUMB MIX

Mix all ingredients together in a bowl until well combined.

*1 quantity*
50 g (2 oz/½ cup)
  breadcrumbs
½ teaspoon salt
¼ teaspoon pepper
1 tablespoon Parmesan cheese,
  grated
1 tablespoon flat leaf parsley,
  finely chopped
1 teaspoon garlic powder

# ACKNOWLEDGEMENTS

Firstly, I must thank the two most influential women in my life of food—my wonderful nonna Maria and my beautiful mum Carmel. These amazing women are the ultimate inspirational foodies in my life who have helped shape my passion and culinary skills. Secondly, I must thank my dedicated dad Anthony for his constant support and guidance, driving me across Melbourne for work in the early days. My talented sister Bianca, without her I wouldn't have compiled this book. My brother Daniel, who found and helped me secure my first full-time work in hospitality and was my personal assistant, taste-testing my work. These family members have always given me the love, support and encouragement to achieve my goals and believe in myself.

Sharyn Johnston, who introduced me to commercial cookery and taught me handy tricks of the trade. My amazing kitchen crew at Vic's Cucina & Bar, especially Robert Dimovski and John Winston Ninon. Without these guys I wouldn't be half as successful. My Food Technology teachers from Salesian College Sunbury, Helen Wright and Pamela Ogilvie. Thanks for the faith and support.

Thanks to my loyal customers for your continued support, who I believe are my true critics. Special thanks to Linda Williams from New Holland Publishers, for all the advice, patience and support.

# MEASUREMENTS

¼ teaspoon = 1.25 ml
½ teaspoon = 2.5 ml
1 teaspoon = 5 ml/5 g
1 tablespoon = 20 ml
Liquid measures: 1 cup = 250 ml (9 fl oz)

# INDEX